Best of
Country
Slow Cooker
RECIPES

Slow Cookers Put You on The Fast Track for Fixing Dinner

IF YOU THINK you can't put a wholesome supper on the table when busy days keep you out of the kitchen, think again! Slow cookers provide unbeatable fix-it-and-forget-it convenience, so you can offer from-scratch fare even on your most hurried days.

Just fill your slow cooker early in the day, turn it on and head out the door. When you come home, you'll be greeted with the wonderful aroma of a simmering dish. By planning ahead, you save time when you need it most.

Best of all, with only one dirty pot, cleanup is a breeze. And if you can't handle the heat in the kitchen, using a slow cooker keeps it cool!

You'll quickly be on your way to enjoying the benefits of slow cooking with this *Best of Country Slow Cooker Recipes*. It's chock-full of 228 great-tasting recipes from past issues of *Taste of Home* and its "sister" publications, so it's a snap to prepare entrees, soups, side dishes, appetizers…even dessert!

You can make every dish with confidence because each one is a tried-and-true favorite of a fellow busy cook. Plus, each recipe has been prepared and taste-tested by our own kitchen staff.

Since some recipes cook all day, while others require only a few hours, we've prominently highlighted the cooking time for each recipe. You can easily select recipes that fit your schedule. (There's also a complete listing of recipes organized by cooking time on page 107 of the index.)

But before you plug in your slow cooker, turn to page 4 for information on making slow cooking even easier and more convenient. Whether you're a new or seasoned slow cooker user, you're sure to appreciate this handy section and the other helpful hints and tips throughout the book.

Soon you'll be enjoying many economical, nutritious and delicious dishes with minimal time and fuss.

This slow cooker's companion is one cookbook you'll turn to time and time again!

Best of Country
Slow Cooker
RECIPES

Editor: Faithann Stoner
Art Director: Niki Malmberg
Food Editor: Janaan Cunningham
Associate Food Editors: Coleen Martin, Diane Werner
Senior Recipe Editor: Sue A. Jurack
Associate Editors: Heidi Reuter Lloyd, Julie Schnittka,
Jean Steiner, Susan Uphill
Food Photography: Rob Hagen, Dan Roberts
Food Photography Artists: Stephanie Marchese,
Vicky Marie Moseley
Photo Studio Manager: Anne Schimmel
Production: Ellen Lloyd, Catherine Fletcher
Publisher: Roy Reiman

Slow Cooker Hints & Tips

Difference Between a Crock-Pot® and a Slow Cooker

THE ORIGINAL slow cooker, called a Crock-Pot, was introduced in 1971 by Rival®. The term "slow cooker" and the name Crock-Pot are frequently used interchangeably when referring to this appliance.

The most popular slow cookers have heat coils circling a crockery insert. With this type, the heat surrounds the food to help it cook evenly.

These models have two heat settings: "high" (equal to 300°F) and "low" (equal to 200°F).

Other types of slow cookers have heat coils on the bottom and have an adjustable thermostat.

All the recipes in this cookbook refer to cooking on either "high" or "low" for a certain amount of time.

When a range in cooking time is provided, this accounts for variables such as thickness of meat, how full the slow cooker is, temperature of the food going into the cooker, etc.

As you become more familiar with your slow cooker, you'll be better able to judge which end of the range to use.

A handy attribute of a slow cooker is that if you can't get home at exactly the time the food should be done, it generally doesn't hurt to leave it cooking on low for an extra hour.

Slow Cooker Basics

- No peeking! Refrain from lifting the lid while the slow cooker is cooking unless you're instructed in a recipe to stir or add ingredients. The loss of steam can mean an additional 15 to 30 minutes of cooking time *each time* you lift the lid.
- Be sure the lid is seated properly—not tilted or askew. The steam during cooking creates a seal.
- Remove food from the slow cooker within 1 hour after it's finished cooking. Promptly refrigerate leftovers.
- Slow cooking may take longer at higher altitudes.

Selecting the Right Slow Cooker Size

SLOW COOKERS come in a range of sizes, from 1 quart to 6 quarts. It's important to use the right size for the amount of food you're making.

To cook properly and safely, manufacturers and the USDA recommend slow cookers be filled at least half full but no more than two-thirds full.

Check the chart below right to find the proper size slow cooker for you.

In general, to serve a dip from a buffet, the smallest slow cookers are ideal. To entertain or cook for a potluck dinner, the larger cookers work best.

Many slow cookers have a removable stoneware insert. That handy feature also allows you to assemble the food the night before, when it's convenient for you. Uncooked meats should be stored separately from other ingredients and added when you're ready to cook.

Cover and store the insert in the refrigerator. Then in the morning, just turn on the cooker, put in the insert and go.

Note: Don't preheat the base unit. An insert that has been in the refrigerator overnight should always be put into a cold base unit. Stoneware is sensitive to dramatic temperature changes and cracking or breakage could occur with preheating.

Another option, especially for recipes that require additional preparation like browning meat, is to assemble your recipe in the evening, put everything in the slow cooker and turn it on. Let it cook overnight while you sleep.

In the morning, when the recipe has cooked for the required amount of time, store your finished dish in the refrigerator and reheat it in the microwave at dinnertime.

Household Size	Size of Slow Cooker (in quarts)
1 person	1 to 1-1/2
2 people	2 to 3-1/2
3 or 4 people	3-1/2 to 4-1/2
4 or 5 people	4-1/2 to 5
6 or more people	5 to 6

Preparing Foods for the Slow Cooker

Meats. For enhanced flavor and appearance, meat may be browned before going into the slow cooker, but it's not necessary. If you decide not to brown the meat, you may want to add color when serving by sprinkling on chopped parsley or shredded cheese. And garnishes such as fresh herbs and lemon wedges can also help.

Vegetables. Vegetables, especially root vegetables like carrots and potatoes, tend to cook slower than meat. Place these vegetables on the bottom and around the sides of the slow cooker and put meat on top of the vegetables. Add tender vegetables like peas and zucchini, or those you'd prefer to be crisp-tender, during the last 15 to 60 minutes.

Dairy. Most milk-based products tend to break down during slow cooking. If possible, add items like milk, sour cream, cream cheese or cream during the last hour of cooking. Cheeses don't generally hold up over extended periods of cooking, so they should be added near the end of cooking—or use processed cheeses instead.

Seasonings. Whole herbs and spices are better than the crushed forms in the slow cooker. The whole berry or leaf is firmer and stands up better over long cooking times. They'll be at their peak at serving time. Add fresh herbs just before the end of cooking.

Beans. Dried beans can be tricky to work with in the slow cooker. Minerals in the water and variations in voltage affect different types of beans in different ways. As a result, dried beans should always be soaked before adding to a slow cooker recipe. Here's how:

Place beans in a Dutch oven or soup kettle; add water to cover by 2 inches. Bring to a boil; boil for 2 minutes. Remove from the heat; cover and let stand for 1 hour. Drain and rinse beans, discarding liquid. **Note:** Lentils and split peas do not need to be soaked. After dried beans are completely cooked, they can be combined with sugar and/or acidic foods, such as tomato sauce. Sugar and acid have a hardening effect on beans and will prevent them from becoming tender. An alternative is to use canned beans that have been rinsed and drained.

Pasta. If added to a slow cooker when dry, pasta becomes very sticky. Partially cook pasta until it's almost tender but not completely cooked before adding. Or, boil it until completely tender and add it at the end of cooking just to heat it through and blend it with the other ingredients.

Fish. Fish is very tender and turns into flakes if slow cooked for long periods. Add fish during the last 20 minutes of cooking.

Converting Recipes for the Slow Cooker

ALMOST ANY RECIPE that bakes in the oven or simmers on the stovetop can be converted for the slow cooker. Here are some guidelines:

Using this book or the manufacturer's instruction booklet, locate a recipe similar to the one you want to convert. Use it as a guide. Note the quantity and size of meat and vegetable pieces, heat setting, cooking time and amount of liquid.

Note: Since there is no evaporation, foods tend to water down. If your recipe calls for 6 to 8 cups of water, you might want to start with 5 cups. Conversely, recipes should include some liquid. If a recipe doesn't include liquid, add a 1/2 cup of water or broth.

In general, 1 hour of simmering on the range or baking at 350° F in the oven is equal to 8-10 hours on low or 4-5 hours on high in a slow cooker. Check the chart at right:

Thickeners such as flour, cornstarch and tomato paste are used to give texture to foods cooked in the slow cooker.

Before converting recipes, check the manufacturer's guidelines for your particular slow cooker.

Cooking Time for Conventional Recipe	Cooking Time in the Slow Cooker
15 to 30 minutes	Low: 4 to 6 hours
	High: 1-1/2 to 2 hours
35 to 45 minutes	Low: 6 to 8 hours
	High: 3 to 4 hours
50 minutes or more	Low: 8 to 10 hours
	High: 4 to 6 hours

Helpful Foil Handles

MEAT LOAVES or layered dishes like Slow Cooker Enchiladas (p. 46) are easier to get out of the slow cooker using foil handles. Here's how:

1. Cut three 20- x 3-inch strips of heavy-duty aluminum foil or create them by folding wider strips of regular foil. Crisscross the strips so they resemble the spokes of a wheel. (See photo 1.)

2. Place the meat loaf in the center of the strips, and pull them up and bend the edges to form handles. (See photo 2.)

3. Grasp the foil handles to lift the loaf and lower it into the slow cooker. (See photo 3.) Leave the foil in while you cook so you can easily lift the meat out to serve.

Note: For a layered dish, place the strips in the cooker and up the sides before putting in the food. Leave them in. Once the food is cooked, pull the strips together as a handle to neatly remove the food in one piece.

1.

2.

3.

Cleaning

REMOVABLE stoneware inserts make cleanup a breeze. Be sure to cool the insert before adding water for cleaning to avoid cracking.

Wash the insert in the dishwasher or in warm soapy water. Avoid using abrasive cleansers since they may scratch the stoneware.

To remove mineral stains on a crockery insert, fill the cooker with hot water and 1 cup white vinegar; cover. Turn heat control to high for 2 hours. Then empty. When cool, wash with hot sudsy water and a cloth or sponge. Rinse well and dry with a towel.

To remove water marks from a highly glazed crockery insert, rub the surface with vegetable oil and allow to stand for 2 hours before washing with hot sudsy water.

Do not immerse the metal base unit. Clean it with a damp sponge.

Special Uses

DON'T FORGET your slow cooker when you go camping, provided electricity is available. It's a handy appliance when space is limited and you want "set-it-and-forget-it" meals.

Reheating foods in a slow cooker is not recommended. Cooked food can be brought to steaming on the stovetop or in the microwave and then put into a preheated slow cooker to keep hot for serving.

Use a slow cooker on a buffet table to keep soup, stew or mashed potatoes hot.

Check to See If Your Slow Cooker Works Properly

INHERIT a used slow cooker or find one at a garage sale and want to see if it's working properly?

To be considered safe, a slow cooker must be able to cook slow enough so that it can be left unattended, yet it must be fast enough to keep the food at a safe temperature. Here's how to check:

1. Fill the slow cooker with 2 quarts of lukewarm water.

2. Heat on low with the lid covered for 8 hours.

3. Using a thermometer, check the temperature of the water quickly since the temperature can drop quite a bit once the lid is removed.

4. The temperature should be at 185° F. If it's too hot, your meal cooked for 8 hours would likely be overdone. If the temperature is below 185°, it could be the cooker does not heat food to an adequate temperature to avoid the growth of harmful bacteria.

Snacks & Beverages

Fruit Salsa (p. 12)
Marinated Chicken Wings (p. 13)

Chapter 1

Slow Cooker Cheese Dip

Cook Time: 4 Hours

Marion Bartone, Conneaut, Ohio

I brought this spicy cheese dip to my quilt guild, where it was a huge hit. It's a terrific take-along appetizer.

  1 pound ground beef
  1/2 pound bulk hot pork sausage
  2 pounds process American cheese, cubed
  2 cans (10 ounces *each*) diced tomatoes and green chilies, undrained
Tortilla chips

In a skillet, cook beef and sausage over medium heat until no longer pink; drain. Transfer to a 5-qt. slow cooker. Add cheese and tomatoes; mix well. Cover and cook on low for 4 hours or until the cheese is melted, stirring occasionally. Serve with tortilla chips. **Yield: 3 quarts.**

Taco Joe Dip

(Pictured below)

Cook Time: 5 to 7 Hours

Lang Secrest, Sierra Vista, Arizona

This recipe was given to us by our daughter. My husband and I absolutely love it. Because it's conveniently prepared in a slow cooker, it's great for parties or busy days.

  1 can (16 ounces) kidney beans, rinsed and drained
  1 can (15-1/4 ounces) whole kernel corn, drained
  1 can (15 ounces) black beans, rinsed and drained
  1 can (14-1/2 ounces) stewed tomatoes

Taco Joe Dip

  1 can (8 ounces) tomato sauce
  1 can (4 ounces) chopped green chilies, drained
  1 envelope taco seasoning
  1/2 cup chopped onion
Tortilla chips

In a slow cooker, combine the first eight ingredients. Cover and cook on low for 5-7 hours. Serve with tortilla chips. **Yield: about 7 cups.**

  Editor's Note: To make Taco Joe Soup, add a 29-ounce can of tomato sauce to the slow cooker. It will serve 6-8.

Hearty Broccoli Dip

Cook Time: 2 to 3 Hours

Sue Call, Beech Grove, Indiana

You'll need just five ingredients to stir up this no-fuss appetizer. People often ask me to bring this creamy dip to potlucks.

  1 pound ground beef
  1 pound process American cheese, cubed
  1 can (10-3/4 ounces) condensed cream of mushroom soup, undiluted
  1 package (10 ounces) frozen chopped broccoli, thawed
  2 tablespoons salsa
Tortilla chips

In a skillet, brown beef; drain. Transfer to a slow cooker. Add cheese, soup, broccoli and salsa; mix well. Cover and cook on low for 2-3 hours or until heated through, stirring after 1 hour. Serve with tortilla chips. **Yield: 5-1/2 cups.**

Cranberry Appetizer Meatballs

Serve in Slow Cooker

Jim Ulberg, Elk Rapids, Michigan

Here's a memorable make-ahead party snack with a tangy non-traditional sauce that includes the flavor of cranberries.

  2 eggs, beaten
  1 cup dry bread crumbs
  1/3 cup minced fresh parsley
  1/3 cup ketchup
  2 tablespoons finely chopped onion
  2 tablespoons soy sauce
  2 garlic cloves, minced
  1/2 teaspoon salt
  1/4 teaspoon pepper
  2 pounds ground beef
SAUCE:
  1 can (16 ounces) whole-berry cranberry sauce
  1 bottle (12 ounces) chili sauce
  1 tablespoon brown sugar
  1 tablespoon prepared mustard
  1 tablespoon lemon juice
  2 garlic cloves, minced

In a bowl, combine the first nine ingredients. Crumble beef over mixture; mix well. Shape into 1-in. balls. Place on a rack in a shallow baking pan. Bake,

Slow-Cooked Salsa

uncovered, at 400° for 15 minutes or until no longer pink. Transfer with a slotted spoon to a slow cooker. Combine sauce ingredients in a saucepan; simmer for 10 minutes, stirring occasionally. Pour over meatballs. Cover and keep warm on low. **Yield:** about 7 dozen.

Pizza Spread

Serve in Slow Cooker

Beverly Mons, Middletown, New York

For a satisfying snack, spread slices of Italian or French bread with this thick cheesy mixture. It's a very adaptable recipe that suits every occasion. It would also be good with Italian sausage instead of ground beef. Kids and adults love it.

   1 pound ground beef
   1 jar (26 ounces) marinara *or* spaghetti sauce
   1 teaspoon dried oregano
   4 cups (16 ounces) shredded mozzarella cheese
   1 loaf Italian *or* French bread, cubed *or* sliced

In a saucepan, cook beef over medium heat until no longer pink; drain. Stir in marinara sauce and oregano. Gradually stir in cheese until melted. Pour into a small slow cooker; cover and keep warm on low. Serve with bread. **Yield:** 8-10 servings.

Slow-Cooked Salsa

(Pictured above)

Cook Time: 2-1/2 to 3 Hours

Toni Menard, Lompoc, California

I love the fresh taste of homemade salsa, but as a working mother, I don't have much time to make it. So I came up with this slow-cooked version that practically makes itself!

  10 plum tomatoes, cored
   2 garlic cloves
   1 small onion, cut into wedges
   2 jalapeno peppers*
  1/4 cup cilantro *or* parsley leaves
  1/2 teaspoon salt

Cut a small slit in two tomatoes; insert a garlic clove into each slit. Place tomatoes and onion in a slow cooker. Cut stem off jalapenos; remove seeds if a milder salsa is desired. Place jalapenos in slow cooker. Cover and cook on high for 2-1/2 to 3 hours or until vegetables are softened (some may brown); cool. In a blender or food processor, combine tomato mixture, cilantro and salt; cover and process until smooth. Refrigerate leftovers. **Yield:** about 2 cups.

  Editor's Note: When cutting or seeding hot peppers, use rubber or plastic gloves to protect your hands. Avoid touching your face.

Hot Chili Dip

Cook Time: 1 to 2 Hours

Nikki Rosati, Franksville, Wisconsin

I first made this zippy dip for my husband's birthday party. Many of our family members and friends asked for the recipe.

   1 jar (24 ounces) salsa
   1 can (15 ounces) chili with beans
   2 cans (2-1/4 ounces *each*) sliced ripe olives, drained
  12 ounces process American cheese, cubed
Tortilla chips

In a small slow cooker, combine the salsa, chili and olives. Stir in cheese. Cover and cook on low for 1-2 hours or until cheese is melted, stirring halfway through. Serve with chips. **Yield:** about 2 cups.

Championship Bean Dip

Championship Bean Dip

(Pictured above)

Cook Time: 2 Hours

Wendi Wavrin Law, Omaha, Nebraska

My friends and neighbors expect me to bring this irresistible dip to every gathering. When I arrive, they ask, "You brought your bean dip, didn't you?" If there are any leftovers, we use them to make bean and cheese burritos the next day. I've given out this recipe a hundred times.

 1 can (16 ounces) refried beans
 1 cup picante sauce
 1 cup (4 ounces) shredded Monterey Jack
    cheese
 1 cup (4 ounces) shredded cheddar cheese
 3/4 cup sour cream
 1 package (3 ounces) cream cheese, softened
 1 tablespoon chili powder
 1/4 teaspoon ground cumin
Tortilla chips and salsa

In a bowl, combine the first eight ingredients; transfer to a slow cooker. Cover and cook on high for 2 hours or until heated through, stirring once or twice. Serve with tortilla chips and salsa. **Yield:** 4-1/2 cups.

Party Sausages

Cook Time: 1 to 2 Hours

Jo Ann Renner, Xenia, Ohio

Don't want any leftovers on January 2? Serve these sausages January 1. I've never had even one end up uneaten. They're so tasty and not tricky to prepare.

 2 pounds fully cooked smoked sausage links
 1 bottle (8 ounces) Catalina salad dressing
 1 bottle (8 ounces) Russian salad dressing

 1/2 cup packed brown sugar
 1/2 cup pineapple juice

Cut sausages diagonally into 1/2-in. slices; cook in a skillet over medium heat until lightly browned. Transfer sausages to a slow cooker; discard drippings. Add dressings, sugar and juice to skillet; cook and stir over medium-low heat until sugar is dissolved. Pour over sausages. Heat on low for 1-2 hours or until heated through. Serve hot. **Yield:** 16 servings.

   Editor's Note: French salad dressing may be substituted for one or both dressings.

All-Day Meatballs

Cook Time: 6 to 8 Hours

Cathy Ryan, Red Wing, Minnesota

Folks who work outside the home can pop these savory meatballs into the slow cooker in the morning. By the time they get home in the evening, dinner's ready!

 1 cup milk
 3/4 cup quick-cooking oats
 3 tablespoons finely chopped onion
1-1/2 teaspoons salt
1-1/2 pounds ground beef
 1 cup ketchup
 1/2 cup water
 3 tablespoons vinegar
 2 tablespoons sugar

In a bowl, combine the first four ingredients. Crumble beef over the mixture and mix well. Shape into 1-in. balls. Place in a slow cooker. In a bowl, combine the ketchup, water, vinegar and sugar; mix well. Pour over meatballs. Cover and cook on low for 6-8 hours or until the meat is no longer pink. **Yield:** 6 servings.

Fruit Salsa

(Pictured at right and on page 8)

Cook Time: 2 Hours

Florence Buchkowsky, Prince Albert, Saskatchewan

Serve this fruity salsa like ordinary salsa. My son and I tried different ingredients to find the best combination. Using the slow cooker minimizes prep time and maximizes the flavor.

 1 can (11 ounces) mandarin oranges,
    undrained
 1 can (8-1/2 ounces) sliced peaches, undrained
 1 can (8 ounces) pineapple tidbits, undrained
 1 medium onion, chopped
 1/2 *each* medium green, sweet red and yellow
    pepper, chopped
 3 garlic cloves, minced
 3 tablespoons cornstarch
 4 teaspoons vinegar
Tortilla chips

In a slow cooker, combine the fruit, onion, peppers, garlic, cornstarch and vinegar; stir well. Cover and cook on high for 2 hours or until thickened and heated through, stirring occasionally. Serve with tortilla chips. **Yield:** 4 cups.

Marinated Chicken Wings

(Pictured below and on page 8)

Cook Time: 3-1/2 to 4 Hours

Janie Botting, Sultan, Washington

I've made these nicely flavored chicken wings many times for get-togethers. They're so moist and tender…and a nice alternative to the spicy wings made with hot pepper sauce.

20 whole chicken wings* (about 4 pounds)
2 cups soy sauce
1/2 cup white wine *or* chicken broth
1/2 cup vegetable oil
2 to 3 garlic cloves, minced
2 tablespoons sugar
2 teaspoons ground ginger

Cut chicken wings into three sections; discard wing tips. Place wings in a large resealable heavy-duty plastic bag or 13-in. x 9-in. x 2-in. baking dish. In a bowl, combine remaining ingredients; mix well. Pour half of the sauce over chicken; turn to coat. Seal or cover the chicken and remaining sauce; refrigerate overnight.

Drain chicken, discarding the marinade. Place the chicken in a 5-qt. slow cooker; top with the reserved sauce. Cover and cook on low for 3-1/2 to 4 hours or until chicken juices run clear. Transfer wings to a serving dish; discard cooking juices. **Yield:** 18-20 servings.

*Editor's Note: 4 pounds of uncooked chicken wing sections may be substituted for the whole wings. Omit the first step of the recipe.

Fruit Salsa
Marinated Chicken Wings

Simmered Smoked Links

Cook Time: 4 Hours

Maxine Cenker, Weirton, West Virginia

A tasty sweet-sour sauce glazes bite-size sausages in this easy recipe. Serve these no-fuss appetizers with toothpicks at parties or holiday get-togethers. I've found that these meaty bites are always popular and never last long.

> **2 packages (16 ounces *each*) miniature smoked sausage links**
> **1 cup packed brown sugar**
> **1/2 cup ketchup**
> **1/4 cup prepared horseradish**

Place sausages in a slow cooker. Mix brown sugar, ketchup and horseradish; pour over sausages. Cover and cook on low for 4 hours. **Yield: 16-20 servings.**

Cheddar Fondue

(Pictured below)

Serve in Slow Cooker

Norene Wright, Manilla, Indiana

This cheesy blend, sparked with mustard and Worcestershire sauce, is a yummy snack.

> **1/4 cup butter *or* margarine**
> **1/4 cup all-purpose flour**
> **1/2 teaspoon salt, optional**
> **1/4 teaspoon pepper**
> **1/4 teaspoon ground mustard**
> **1/4 teaspoon Worcestershire sauce**
> **1-1/2 cups milk**
> **2 cups (8 ounces) shredded cheddar cheese**
> **Bread cubes, ham cubes, bite-size sausage *and/or* broccoli florets**

Cheddar Fondue

In a saucepan, melt butter; stir in flour, salt if desired, pepper, mustard and Worcestershire sauce until smooth. Gradually add milk. Bring to a boil; cook and stir for 2 minutes or until thickened. Reduce heat. Add the cheese; cook and stir until melted. Transfer to a slow cooker; cover and keep warm on low. Serve with bread, ham, sausage and/or broccoli. **Yield: 2-1/2 cups.**

Reuben Spread

Cook Time: 3 Hours

Pam Rohr, Troy, Ohio

You'll need only five ingredients to stir up this hearty dip that tastes amazingly like a Reuben sandwich. Everyone goes back for seconds. It's a deliciously different snack.

> **2-1/2 cups cubed cooked corned beef**
> **1 jar (16 ounces) sauerkraut, rinsed and well drained**
> **2 cups (8 ounces) shredded Swiss cheese**
> **2 cups (8 ounces) shredded cheddar cheese**
> **1 cup mayonnaise***
> **Snack rye bread**

In a slow cooker, combine the first five ingredients and mix well. Cover and cook on low for 3 hours, stirring occasionally. Serve warm with rye bread. **Yield: about 5 cups.**

*Editor's Note: Reduced-fat cheese and mayonnaise are not recommended for this recipe.

Nacho Rice Dip

Serve in Slow Cooker

Audra Hungate, Holt, Missouri

Spanish rice mix adds an interesting twist to this effortless appetizer. Every time I serve this dip at gatherings with family members and friends, my guests gobble it up. It's a hearty snack that really satisfies.

> **1 package (6.8 ounces) Spanish rice and vermicelli mix**
> **2 tablespoons butter *or* margarine**
> **2 cups water**
> **1 can (14-1/2 ounces) diced tomatoes, undrained**
> **1 pound ground beef**
> **1 pound (16 ounces) process American cheese, cubed**
> **1 can (14-1/2 ounces) stewed tomatoes**
> **1 jar (8 ounces) process cheese sauce**
> **Tortilla chips**

In a large saucepan, cook rice mix in butter until golden. Stir in water and diced tomatoes; bring to a boil. Reduce heat; cover and simmer for 15-20 minutes or until rice is tender. Meanwhile, in a skillet, cook beef until no longer pink. Drain and add to the rice. Stir in cheese, stewed tomatoes and cheese sauce; cook and stir until cheese is melted. Transfer to a slow cooker; cover and keep warm on low. Serve with tortilla chips. **Yield: about 8 cups.**

Slow Cooker Party Mix
Hot Crab Dip

Hot Crab Dip

(Pictured above)

Cook Time: 3 to 4 Hours

Teri Rasey-Bolf, Cadillac, Michigan

I have six children and one grandchild, work full-time and coach soccer and football. I appreciate recipes like this that are easy to assemble. The rich creamy dip is an appetizer that always goes over well during the holidays.

　1/2 cup milk
　1/3 cup salsa
　　3 packages (8 ounces *each*) cream cheese, cubed
　　2 packages (8 ounces *each*) imitation crabmeat, flaked
　　1 cup thinly sliced green onions
　　1 can (4 ounces) chopped green chilies
Assorted crackers

Combine milk and salsa. Transfer to a slow cooker coated with nonstick cooking spray. Stir in cream cheese, crab, onions and chilies. Cover and cook on low for 3-4 hours, stirring every 30 minutes. Serve with crackers. **Yield:** about 5 cups.

Slow Cooker Party Mix

(Pictured above)

Cook Time: 3 Hours

Dana Hughes, Gresham, Oregon

This mildly seasoned snack mix is always a party favorite. The munchable mixture is very satisfying, especially when it's served warm from a slow cooker, which makes it extra special. When I set out this mix, people tend to gather at the snack table.

　　4 cups Wheat Chex
　　4 cups Cheerios
　　3 cups pretzel sticks
　　1 can (12 ounces) salted peanuts
　1/4 cup butter *or* margarine, melted
　　2 to 3 tablespoons grated Parmesan cheese
　　1 teaspoon celery salt
　1/2 to 3/4 teaspoon seasoned salt

In a 5-qt. slow cooker, combine cereals, pretzels and peanuts. Combine butter, Parmesan cheese, celery salt and seasoned salt; drizzle over cereal mixture and mix well. Cover and cook on low for up to 3 hours, stirring every 30 minutes. Serve warm or at room temperature. **Yield:** about 3 quarts.

Spiced Apricot Cider

1/2 teaspoon anise extract
4 cinnamon sticks (3 inches), halved
1-1/2 teaspoons whole cloves
Additional cinnamon sticks, optional

In a slow cooker, combine the first four ingredients; mix well. Place cinnamon sticks and cloves in a double thickness of cheesecloth; bring up corners of cloth and tie with string to form a bag. Add to slow cooker. Cover and cook on low for 2-3 hours. Discard spice bag. Ladle coffee into mugs; garnish each with a cinnamon stick if desired. **Yield:** 8 cups.

Mulled Grape Cider

Cook Time: 3 Hours

Sharon Harmon, Orange, Massachusetts

I created this recipe one year when I tried to make grape jelly and ended up with jars of grape syrup instead. Knowing that people like hot apple cider, I simmered the syrup with spices to make a beverage. My friends raved over it.

> 5 pounds Concord grapes
> 8 cups water, *divided*
> 1-1/2 cups sugar
> 8 whole cloves
> 4 cinnamon sticks (4 inches)
> Dash ground nutmeg

In a large saucepan or Dutch oven, combine grapes and 2 cups water; bring to a boil, stirring constantly. Press through a strainer; reserve juice and discard skins and seeds. Pour juice through a double layer of cheesecloth into a slow cooker. Add sugar, cloves, cinnamon sticks, nutmeg and remaining water. Heat on low for 3 hours. Discard cloves and cinnamon sticks before serving. **Yield:** 10-12 servings (2-3/4 quarts).

Spiced Apricot Cider

(Pictured above)

Cook Time: 2 Hours

Connie Cummings, Gloucester, New Jersey

You'll need just six ingredients to simmer together this hot spiced beverage. Each delicious mugful is rich with apricot flavor.

> 2 cans (12 ounces *each*) apricot nectar
> 2 cups water
> 1/4 cup lemon juice
> 1/4 cup sugar
> 2 whole cloves
> 2 cinnamon sticks (3 inches)
> Additional cinnamon sticks, optional

In a slow cooker, combine all ingredients; mix well. Cover and cook on low for 2 hours or until cider reaches desired temperature. Remove cloves and cinnamon sticks before serving. Garnish each cup with a cinnamon stick if desired. **Yield:** 6 servings.

Spiced Coffee

(Pictured at right)

Cook Time: 2 to 3 Hours

Joanne Holt, Bowling Green, Ohio

Even those who usually don't drink coffee will find this spiced blend with a hint of chocolate appealing. I keep a big batch simmering when I host a brunch or open house.

> 8 cups brewed coffee
> 1/3 cup sugar
> 1/4 cup chocolate syrup

Spiced Coffee

Hot Cranberry Punch

(Pictured at right)

Cook Time: 2 to 3 Hours

Laura Burgess, Ballwin, Missouri

I serve this rosy spiced beverage at parties and family gatherings during the winter. Friends like the tangy twist it gets from red-hot candies. It's a nice change from the usual hot chocolate.

    8 cups hot water
1-1/2 cups sugar
    4 cups cranberry juice
  3/4 cup orange juice
  1/4 cup lemon juice
   12 whole cloves, optional
  1/2 cup red-hot candies

In a 5-qt. slow cooker, combine water, sugar and juices; stir until sugar is dissolved. If desired, place cloves in a double thickness of cheesecloth; bring up corners of cloth and tie with string to form a bag. Add spice bag and red-hots to slow cooker. Cover and cook on low for 2-3 hours or until heated though. Before serving, discard spice bag and stir punch. **Yield:** 3-1/2 quarts.

Peachy Spiced Cider

Cook Time: 4 to 6 Hours

Rose Harman, Hays, Kansas

It's nice to welcome guests with the inviting aroma of this warm beverage. I served this spiced cider at a Christmas cookie exchange and received many compliments. Everyone seemed to enjoy the subtle peach flavor.

    4 cans (5-1/2 ounces *each*) peach nectar
    2 cups apple juice
  1/4 to 1/2 teaspoon ground ginger
  1/4 teaspoon ground cinnamon
  1/4 teaspoon ground nutmeg
    4 fresh orange slices (1/4 inch thick), halved

Combine the first five ingredients in a slow cooker. Top with the orange slices. Cover and cook on low for 4-6 hours or until heated through. Stir before serving. **Yield:** about 1 quart.

Hot Citrus Cider

Cook Time: 2 to 4 Hours

Catherine Allan, Twin Falls, Idaho

I first tasted a steaming mug of this comforting beverage on a chilly evening. It's still a family favorite on a wintry day. We love the mix of fruit juices and subtle sweetness and spice.

    2 quarts apple cider
    1 cup pineapple juice
    1 cup orange juice
    1 tablespoon brown sugar
    1 tablespoon lemon juice
  1/8 teaspoon salt
    8 whole cloves

Hot Cranberry Punch

    4 unpeeled fresh orange slices (1/4 inch thick)
    4 cinnamon sticks (3 inches)

In a slow cooker, combine the first six ingredients. Push two cloves through each orange slice. Push a cinnamon stick through the center of each orange slice; add to cider mixture. Cover and cook on low for 2-4 hours or until heated through. Discard oranges, cloves and cinnamon sticks. Stir cider before serving. **Yield:** 2-1/2 quarts.

Slow Cooker Cider

Cook Time: 2 to 5 Hours

Alpha Wilson, Roswell, New Mexico

Family and friends feel warmly welcomed when they enjoy the aroma and flavor of this wonderful warm cider. Best of all, slow cooking means no last-minute rush.

    2 cinnamon sticks (4 inches)
    1 teaspoon whole cloves
    1 teaspoon whole allspice
    2 quarts apple cider
  1/2 cup packed brown sugar
    1 medium orange, sliced

Place cinnamon, cloves and allspice in a double thickness of cheesecloth; bring up the corners of cloth and tie with a string to form a bag. Place cider and brown sugar in a slow cooker; stir until sugar dissolves. Add spice bag. Place orange slices on top. Cover and cook on low for 2-5 hours. Remove spice bag before serving. **Yield:** 2 quarts.

This Bark Is Worth a Bite

Cinnamon is actually the inner bark of a tropical evergreen tree. The bark is collected during the rainy season when it's most pliable. When dried, it curls into long quills. Then it is either cut into lengths and sold as cinnamon sticks or ground into powdered cinnamon.

Hearty Soups & Stews

Slow Cooker Vegetable Soup (p. 23)

Chapter 2

Slow-Cooked Sauerkraut Soup

(Pictured below)

Cook Time: 5 to 6 Hours

Linda Lohr, Lititz, Pennsylvania

We live in Lancaster County, Pennsylvania, which has a rich heritage of German culture. Dishes that include sauerkraut, potatoes and sausage abound here. We enjoy this recipe on cold winter evenings, along with muffins and fruit. The "mmm's" start with the first whiff as the door opens after school or work.

- 1 medium potato, cut into 1/4-inch cubes
- 1 pound smoked kielbasa, cut into 1/2-inch cubes
- 1 can (32 ounces) sauerkraut, rinsed and drained
- 4 cups chicken broth
- 1 can (10-3/4 ounces) condensed cream of mushroom soup, undiluted
- 1/2 pound fresh mushrooms, sliced
- 1 cup cubed cooked chicken
- 2 medium carrots, cut into 1/4-inch slices
- 2 celery ribs, sliced
- 2 tablespoons vinegar
- 2 teaspoons dill weed
- 1/2 teaspoon pepper
- 3 to 4 bacon strips, cooked and crumbled

In a 5-qt. slow cooker, combine the first 12 ingredients. Cover and cook on high for 5-6 hours or until the vegetables are tender. Skim fat. Garnish individual servings with bacon. **Yield:** 10-12 servings (about 3 quarts).

Slow-Cooked Sauerkraut Soup

White Chili

Cook Time: 8 to10 Hours

Lana Rutledge, Shepherdsville, Kentucky

This savory white chili simmers all day on the kitchen countertop. So when your hungry clan calls for dinner, you can ladle up steaming bowlfuls in a hurry. It's a wonderful alternative to traditional tomato-based chilies.

- 2 medium onions, chopped
- 4 garlic cloves, minced
- 2 quarts water
- 3 pounds chicken breasts *or* thighs, skin removed
- 1 pound dry navy beans
- 2 cans (4 ounces *each*) chopped green chilies
- 1 tablespoon ground cumin
- 2 teaspoons dried oregano
- 1 teaspoon salt
- 1/2 to 1 teaspoon cayenne pepper
- 1/2 teaspoon ground cloves
- 2 chicken bouillon cubes

Shredded Monterey Jack cheese
Sour cream
Dried chives and crushed red pepper flakes

Place the onions and garlic in a slow cooker. Add the next 10 ingredients; do not stir. Cook on high for 8-10 hours. Uncover and stir (the meat should fall off the bones). Remove bones. Stir to break up the meat. Spoon into bowls; top with cheese and sour cream if desired, and sprinkle with chives and red pepper flakes. **Yield:** 12 servings (3 quarts).

Smoked Sausage Soup

Cook Time: 5 to 8 Hours

Rachel Lyn Grasmick, Rocky Ford, Colorado

This rich soup is packed with vegetables, sausage and chicken. I guarantee it's unlike any other soup you've ever tasted.

- 2 cups chopped onion
- 2 tablespoons butter *or* margarine
- 2 cups cubed cooked chicken
- 1 pound cooked smoked sausage, cut into bite-size pieces
- 3 cups sliced celery
- 3 cups sliced summer squash
- 2 cups chicken broth
- 1-1/2 cups minced fresh parsley
- 1 can (8 ounces) tomato sauce
- 2 tablespoons cornstarch
- 2 tablespoons poultry seasoning
- 1 teaspoon dried oregano
- 1 teaspoon ground cumin
- 1 teaspoon liquid smoke, optional
- 1/2 teaspoon pepper

In a skillet or microwave, cook onion in butter until softened. Transfer to a 3-qt. or larger slow cooker. Add remaining ingredients, stirring to blend. Cook on high for 5-8 hours. **Yield:** 6-8 servings (2-1/2 quarts).

No-Fuss Potato Soup

No-Fuss Potato Soup

(Pictured above)

Cook Time: 7 to 8 Hours

Dotty Egge, Pelican Rapids, Minnesota

For a busy-day supper, my family loves to have big steaming, scrumptious bowls of this hearty soup, along with fresh bread from our bread machine.

> 6 cups cubed peeled potatoes
> 5 cups water
> 2 cups chopped onion
> 1/2 cup chopped celery
> 1/2 cup thinly sliced carrots
> 1/4 cup butter *or* margarine
> 4 teaspoons chicken bouillon granules
> 2 teaspoons salt
> 1/4 teaspoon pepper
> 1 can (12 ounces) evaporated milk
> 3 tablespoons chopped fresh parsley
Snipped chives, optional

In a large slow cooker, combine the first nine ingredients. Cover and cook on high for 7-8 hours or until the vegetables are tender. Add milk and parsley; mix well. Cover and cook 30-60 minutes longer or until heated through. Garnish with chives if desired. **Yield:** 8-10 servings (about 3 quarts).

Forgotten Minestrone

Cook Time: 7-1/2 to 10 Hours

Marsha Ransom, South Haven, Michigan

As a freelance writer, I can be composing an article while a pot of full-flavored soup is simmering. I sprinkle servings with Parmesan cheese and serve this soup with garlic bread.

> 1 pound lean beef stew meat
> 6 cups water
> 1 can (28 ounces) tomatoes with liquid, cut up
> 1 beef bouillon cube
> 1 medium onion, chopped
> 2 tablespoons minced dried parsley
2-1/2 teaspoons salt

> 1-1/2 teaspoons ground thyme
> 1/2 teaspoon pepper
> 1 medium zucchini, thinly sliced
> 2 cups finely chopped cabbage
> 1 can (16 ounces) garbanzo beans, drained
> 1 cup uncooked small elbow *or* shell macaroni
> 1/4 cup grated Parmesan cheese, optional

In a slow cooker, combine beef, water, tomatoes, bouillon, onion, parsley, salt, thyme and pepper. Cover and cook on low for 7-9 hours or until meat is tender. Add zucchini, cabbage, beans and macaroni; cook on high, covered, 30-45 minutes more or until the vegetables are tender. Sprinkle individual servings with Parmesan cheese if desired. **Yield:** 8 servings.

Rich French Onion Soup

(Pictured below)

Cook Time: 5 to 7 Hours

Linda Adolph, Edmonton, Alberta

When entertaining guests, I bring out this tried-and-true soup while we're waiting for the main course. It's simple to make—just saute the onions early in the day and let the soup simmer until dinnertime. In the winter, big bowls of it make a warming supper with a salad and biscuits.

> 6 large onions, chopped
> 1/2 cup butter *or* margarine
> 6 cans (10-1/2 ounces *each*) condensed beef broth, undiluted
> 1-1/2 teaspoons Worcestershire sauce
> 3 bay leaves
> 10 slices French bread, toasted
Shredded Parmesan and mozzarella cheeses

In a large skillet, saute onions in butter until crisp-tender. Transfer to an ungreased 5-qt. slow cooker. Add the broth, Worcestershire sauce and bay leaves. Cover and cook on low for 5-7 hours or until the onions are tender. Discard bay leaves. Top each serving with French bread and cheeses. **Yield:** 10 servings.

Rich French Onion Soup

Chili in Bread Bowls

(Pictured below)

Cook Time: 7 to 8 Hours

Nancy Clancy, Standish, Maine

Some say you can have your cake and eat it, too…I say eat your chili and the bowl, too! I work the "graveyard shift" at the post office in Portland. During those hours, there is no place to buy meals, so I often bring in dishes like this.

- 1 tablespoon all-purpose flour
- 1/4 teaspoon salt
- 1/8 teaspoon pepper
- 1/2 pound *each* lean beef stew meat, boneless skinless chicken breast and boneless pork, cut into cubes
- 1 tablespoon vegetable oil
- 1 medium onion, chopped
- 1 medium green pepper, chopped
- 1 jalapeno pepper, seeded and chopped*
- 1 can (28 ounces) diced tomatoes, drained
- 1 can (16 ounces) kidney beans, rinsed and drained
- 1 can (15-1/2 ounces) navy beans *or* great northern beans, rinsed and drained
- 1 can (8 ounces) tomato sauce
- 1 tablespoon chili powder
- 1 garlic clove, minced
- 1-1/2 teaspoons ground cumin
- 1/2 teaspoon dried basil
- 1/4 to 1/2 teaspoon cayenne pepper
- 9 large hard rolls
- Sour cream, chopped green onions and sweet red pepper, optional

In a large resealable plastic bag, combine the flour, salt and pepper. Add meat in batches; toss to coat. In a large skillet, brown meat in oil in batches. Transfer to a 5-qt. slow cooker with a slotted spoon. Stir in onion, peppers, tomatoes, beans, tomato sauce and seasonings. Cover and cook on low for 7-8 hours or until meat is tender. Cut tops off rolls; carefully hollow out bottom halves. Spoon about 1 cup of chili into each roll. Garnish with sour cream, onions and red pepper if desired. **Yield:** 9 servings.

*Editor's Note: When cutting or seeding hot peppers, use rubber or plastic gloves to protect your hands. Avoid touching your face.

Barbecued Beef Chili

Cook Time: 6 to 7 Hours

Phyllis Shyan, Elgin, Illinois

Served with bread and a side salad, this beefy chili makes a hearty meal. The recipe was inspired by two friends when we were talking about food at a potluck barbecue.

- 7 teaspoons chili powder
- 1 tablespoon garlic powder
- 2 teaspoons celery seed
- 1 teaspoon coarsely ground pepper
- 1/4 to 1/2 teaspoon cayenne pepper
- 1 fresh beef brisket* (3 to 4 pounds)
- 1 medium green pepper, chopped
- 1 small onion, chopped
- 1 bottle (12 ounces) chili sauce
- 1 cup ketchup
- 1/2 cup barbecue sauce
- 1/3 cup packed brown sugar
- 1/4 cup cider vinegar
- 1/4 cup Worcestershire sauce
- 1 teaspoon ground mustard
- 1 can (15-1/2 ounces) hot chili beans
- 1 can (15-1/2 ounces) great northern beans, rinsed and drained

Combine the first five ingredients; rub over brisket. Cut into eight pieces; place in a slow cooker. Combine green pepper, onion, chili sauce, ketchup, barbecue sauce, brown sugar, vinegar, Worcestershire sauce and mustard; pour over meat. Cover and cook on high for 5-6 hours or until meat is tender.

Remove meat; cool slightly. Meanwhile, skim fat from cooking juices. Shred meat with two forks; return to slow cooker. Reduce heat to low. Stir in the beans. Cover and cook for 1 hour or until heated through. **Yield:** 12 servings.

*Editor's Note: This is a fresh beef brisket, not corned beef.

Hominy Pork Soup

Cook Time: 4 Hours

Raquel Walkup, San Pedro, California

Tender pork and hominy make this chili-like soup different from the usual offerings. For a satisfying supper, serve it with sliced green onions, shredded cheese, lime wedges and flour tortillas.

- 1 pound pork chop suey meat, cut into 1/2-inch cubes

Chili in Bread Bowls

2 cans (15 ounces *each*) chili without beans
1 can (15-1/2 ounces) hominy, drained
1 can (8 ounces) tomato sauce
1 medium onion, chopped
1 bay leaf
1 tablespoon chili powder
1 teaspoon *each* dried basil, oregano and
   parsley flakes
1 teaspoon ground cumin
Warmed flour tortillas, shredded Monterey Jack
   cheese, sliced green onions and lime wedges,
   optional

In a slow cooker, combine the pork, chili, hominy, tomato sauce, onion and seasonings. Cover and cook on high for 4 hours or until meat is tender. Discard bay leaf. Serve with tortillas, cheese, green onions and lime wedges if desired. **Yield:** 7 servings.

Trout Chowder

(Pictured below)

Cook Time: 1-1/2 to 2 Hours

Linda Kesselring, Corning, New York

This hearty chowder cooks conveniently in a slow cooker, so I can spend more time fishing and less in the kitchen. Broccoli adds fresh taste and lively color to the rich cheesy broth.

1 medium onion, chopped
1 tablespoon butter *or* margarine
2 cups milk
1 cup ranch salad dressing
1 pound boneless trout fillets, skin removed
1 package (10 ounces) frozen broccoli cuts,
   thawed
1 cup cubed *or* shredded cheddar cheese
1 cup cubed *or* shredded Monterey Jack cheese
1/4 teaspoon garlic powder
Paprika, optional

Slow Cooker Vegetable Soup

In a skillet, saute onion in butter until tender. Transfer to a slow cooker; add milk, dressing, fish, broccoli, cheeses and garlic powder. Cover and cook on high for 1-1/2 to 2 hours or until soup is bubbly and fish flakes easily with a fork. Sprinkle with paprika if desired. **Yield:** 6 servings.

Slow Cooker Vegetable Soup

(Pictured above and on page 18)

Cook Time: 8 Hours

Heather Thurmeier, Pense, Saskatchewan

What a treat it is to come home from work and have this satisfying soup simmering away. It's a nice traditional beef soup with old-fashioned goodness. We pair it with fresh crusty rolls topped with melted mozzarella cheese.

1 pound boneless round steak, cut into
   1/2-inch cubes
1 can (14-1/2 ounces) diced tomatoes,
   undrained
3 cups water
2 medium potatoes, peeled and cubed
2 medium onions, diced
3 celery ribs, sliced
2 carrots, sliced
3 beef bouillon cubes
1/2 teaspoon dried basil
1/2 teaspoon dried oregano
1/2 teaspoon salt
1/4 teaspoon pepper
1-1/2 cups frozen mixed vegetables

In a slow cooker, combine the first 12 ingredients. Cover and cook on high for 6 hours. Add vegetables; cover and cook on high 2 hours longer or until the meat and vegetables are tender. **Yield:** 8-10 servings (about 2-1/2 quarts).

Trout Chowder

Texican Chili

Manhattan Clam Chowder

Cook Time: 8 to 10 Hours

Mary Dixon, Northville, Michigan

I came up with this simple, delicious soup years ago when my husband and I both worked. It's easy to dump all the ingredients into the slow cooker first thing in the morning...and wonderful to come home to the aroma of dinner ready. I like to serve it with bread and a salad.

     3 celery ribs, sliced
     1 large onion, chopped
     1 can (14-1/2 ounces) sliced potatoes, drained
     1 can (14-1/2 ounces) sliced carrots, drained
     2 cans (6-1/2 ounces *each*) chopped clams
     2 cups tomato juice
1-1/2 cups water
   1/2 cup tomato puree
     1 tablespoon dried parsley flakes
1-1/2 teaspoons dried thyme
     1 teaspoon salt
     1 bay leaf
     2 whole black peppercorns

In a slow cooker, combine all ingredients; stir. Cover and cook on low for 8-10 hours or until the vegetables are tender. Remove bay leaf and peppercorns before serving. **Yield:** 9 servings.

Texican Chili

(Pictured above)

Cook Time: 9 to 10 Hours

Stacy Law, Cornish, Utah

This flavorful, meaty chili is my favorite...and it's so easy to prepare in the slow cooker. It's a great way to serve a crowd without last-minute preparation. I got the idea from my mother, who used her slow cooker often for soups and stews.

     8 bacon strips, diced
2-1/2 pounds beef stew meat, cut into
       1/2-inch cubes
     2 cans (one 28 ounces, one 14-1/2 ounces)
       stewed tomatoes
     2 cans (8 ounces *each*) tomato sauce
     1 can (16 ounces) kidney beans, rinsed
       and drained
     2 cups sliced carrots
     1 medium onion, chopped
     1 cup chopped celery
   1/2 cup chopped green pepper
   1/4 cup minced fresh parsley
     1 tablespoon chili powder
     1 teaspoon salt
   1/2 teaspoon ground cumin
   1/4 teaspoon pepper

In a skillet, cook bacon until crisp. Remove to paper towel to drain. Brown beef in the drippings over medium heat; drain. Transfer to a 5-qt. slow cooker; add bacon and remaining ingredients. Cover and cook on low for 9-10 hours or until the meat is tender, stirring occasionally. **Yield:** 16-18 servings.

Hearty Bean Soup

(Pictured below)

Cook Time: 6 to 7 Hours

Alice Schnoor, Arion, Iowa

This thick soup, with dried beans, ham and vegetables, is a tasty main dish or a satisfying first course.

     3 cups chopped parsnips
     2 cups chopped carrots

Hearty Bean Soup

1 cup chopped onion
1-1/2 cups dry great northern beans
5 cups water
1-1/2 pounds smoked ham hocks *or* ham shanks
2 garlic cloves, minced
2 teaspoons salt
1/2 teaspoon pepper
1/8 to 1/4 teaspoon hot pepper sauce

In a 5-qt. slow cooker, place parsnips, carrots and onion. Top with beans. Add water, ham, garlic, salt, pepper and hot pepper sauce. Cover and cook on high for 6-7 hours or until beans are tender. Remove meat and bones when cool enough to handle. Cut meat into bite-size pieces and return to slow cooker; heat through. **Yield:** 6 servings.

Meaty Tomato Soup

Cook Time: 8 Hours

Ann Bost, Elkhart, Texas

As an elementary school librarian and church choir director, I've come to rely on and thoroughly enjoy slow-cooked meals. A sorority sister shared this recipe with me.

1 can (28 ounces) diced tomatoes, undrained
2 cans (8 ounces *each*) tomato sauce
2 cups water
1/2 pound ground beef, cooked and drained
1/2 pound bulk pork sausage, cooked and drained
2 tablespoons dried minced onion
2 chicken bouillon cubes
3/4 teaspoon garlic salt
3/4 cup uncooked elbow macaroni
Shredded cheddar cheese, optional

In a slow cooker, combine the first eight ingredients; mix well. Cover and cook on low for 8 hours. Add macaroni and mix well. Cover and cook 15 minutes longer or until macaroni is tender. Garnish with cheese if desired. **Yield:** 8-10 servings (2-1/4 quarts).

Summer's Bounty Soup

Cook Time: 7 to 8 Hours

Victoria Zmarzley-Hahn, Northampton, Pennsylvania

Lots of wonderfully fresh-tasting vegetables are showcased in this chunky soup. It's a great way to use up summer's excess produce. And it's so versatile—you can add or delete any vegetable.

4 medium tomatoes, chopped
2 medium potatoes, peeled and cubed
2 cups halved fresh green beans
2 small zucchini, cubed
1 medium yellow summer squash, cubed
4 small carrots, thinly sliced
2 celery ribs, thinly sliced
1 cup cubed peeled eggplant
1 cup sliced fresh mushrooms

1 small onion, chopped
1 tablespoon minced fresh parsley
1 tablespoon salt-free garlic and herb seasoning
4 cups V8 juice

Combine all ingredients in a 5-qt. slow cooker. Cover and cook on low for 7-8 hours or until the vegetables are tender. **Yield:** 12-14 servings (about 3-1/2 quarts).

Potato Chowder

(Pictured below)

Cook Time: 8 to 10 Hours

Anna Mayer, Ft. Branch, Indiana

One of the ladies in our church quilting group brought this savory potato soup to a meeting. It's easy to assemble in the morning, then cook all day. Cream cheese and a sprinkling of bacon provide richness.

8 cups diced potatoes
1/3 cup chopped onion
3 cans (14-1/2 ounces *each*) chicken broth
1 can (10-3/4 ounces) condensed cream of chicken soup, undiluted
1/4 teaspoon pepper
1 package (8 ounces) cream cheese, cubed
1/2 pound sliced bacon, cooked and crumbled, optional
Snipped chives, optional

In a slow cooker, combine the first five ingredients. Cover and cook on low for 8-10 hours or until potatoes are tender. Add cream cheese; stir until blended. Garnish with bacon and chives if desired. **Yield:** 12 servings (3 quarts).

Potato Chowder

Seafood Chowder

Cook Time: 4 to 5 Hours

Marlene Muckenhirn, Delano, Minnesota

Our family requests this creamy chowder for Christmas Eve supper. It's an easy-to-serve and easy-to-clean-up meal between our church service and gift exchange.

- 1 can (10-3/4 ounces) condensed cream of potato soup, undiluted
- 1 can (10-3/4 ounces) condensed cream of mushroom soup, undiluted
- 2-1/2 cups milk
- 4 medium carrots, finely chopped
- 2 medium potatoes, peeled and cut into 1/4-inch cubes
- 1 large onion, finely chopped
- 2 celery ribs, finely chopped
- 1 can (6-1/2 ounces) chopped clams, drained
- 1 can (6 ounces) medium shrimp, drained
- 4 ounces imitation crabmeat, flaked
- 5 bacon strips, cooked and crumbled

In a slow cooker, combine soups and milk. Stir in the vegetables. Cover and cook on low for 4-5 hours. Stir in clams, shrimp and crab; cover and heat through, about 20 minutes. Garnish each serving with bacon. **Yield:** 8 servings.

Beef 'n' Black Bean Soup

(Pictured below)

Cook Time: 6 to 7 Hours

Vickie Gibson, Gardendale, Alabama

I lead a busy life, so I'm always trying to come up with time-saving recipes. This zesty and colorful soup is one of my husband's favorites. It has been a hit at family gatherings, too.

- 1 pound ground beef
- 2 cans (14-1/2 ounces each) chicken broth

Beef 'n' Black Bean Soup

- 1 can (14-1/2 ounces) diced tomatoes, undrained
- 8 green onions, thinly sliced
- 3 medium carrots, thinly sliced
- 2 celery ribs, thinly sliced
- 2 garlic cloves, minced
- 1 tablespoon sugar
- 1-1/2 teaspoons dried basil
- 1/2 teaspoon salt
- 1/2 teaspoon dried oregano
- 1/2 teaspoon ground cumin
- 1/2 teaspoon chili powder
- 2 cans (15 ounces each) black beans, rinsed and drained
- 1-1/2 cups cooked rice

In a skillet over medium heat, cook beef until no longer pink; drain. Transfer to a slow cooker. Add the next 12 ingredients. Cover and cook on high for 1 hour. Reduce heat to low; cook for 4-5 hours or until vegetables are tender. Add the beans and rice; cook 1 hour longer or until heated through. **Yield:** 10 servings (2-1/2 quarts).

Buffalo Chicken Wing Soup

Cook Time: 4 to 5 Hours

Pat Farmer, Falconer, New York

My husband and I love buffalo chicken wings, so we created a soup with the same zippy flavor. It's very popular with guests. Start with a small amount of hot sauce, then add more if needed to suit your family's tastes.

- 6 cups milk
- 3 cans (10-3/4 ounces each) condensed cream of chicken soup, undiluted
- 3 cups shredded cooked chicken (about 1 pound)
- 1 cup (8 ounces) sour cream
- 1/4 to 1/2 cup hot pepper sauce

Combine all ingredients in a slow cooker. Cover and cook on low for 4-5 hours. **Yield:** 8 servings (2 quarts).

Spicy Beef Vegetable Soup

Cook Time: 8 Hours

Lynnette Davis, Tullahoma, Tennessee

This savory ground beef and vegetable soup is flavorful and fast to fix. It makes a complete meal when served with warm corn bread, sourdough bread or French bread.

- 1 pound ground beef
- 1 cup chopped onion
- 1 jar (30 ounces) meatless spaghetti sauce
- 3-1/2 cups water
- 1 package (16 ounces) frozen mixed vegetables
- 1 can (10 ounces) diced tomatoes and green chilies
- 1 cup sliced celery
- 1 teaspoon beef bouillon granules
- 1 teaspoon pepper

In a skillet over medium heat, cook beef and onion until meat is no longer pink; drain. Transfer to a slow cooker. Stir in the remaining ingredients. Cover and cook on low for 8 hours or until the vegetables are tender. **Yield:** 12 servings (3 quarts).

Slow-Cooked Chunky Chili

(Pictured at right)

Cook Time: 4 to 5 Hours

Margie Shaw, Greenbrier, Arkansas

Pork sausage, ground beef and plenty of beans make this chili a hearty meal-starter. I serve bowls of it on cold days—or use it to fix chili dogs, tacos and more.

     1 pound ground beef
     1 pound bulk pork sausage
     4 cans (16 ounces *each*) kidney beans, rinsed
        and drained
     2 cans (14-1/2 ounces *each*) diced tomatoes,
        undrained
     2 cans (10 ounces *each*) diced tomatoes and
        green chilies, undrained
     1 large onion, chopped
     1 medium green pepper, chopped
     1 envelope taco seasoning
  1/2 teaspoon salt
  1/4 teaspoon pepper

In a skillet, cook beef and sausage over medium heat until meat is no longer pink; drain. Transfer to a 5-qt. slow cooker. Stir in the remaining ingredients. Cover and cook on high for 4-5 hours or until vegetables are tender. **Yield:** 3 quarts (12 servings).

Potato Minestrone

Cook Time: 8 Hours

Paula Zsiray, Logan, Utah

I only have to slice some bread, prepare a salad and serve this flavorful soup to have dinner ready. For a thicker soup, mash half of the garbanzo beans before adding them to the slow cooker.

     2 cans (14-1/2 ounces *each*) chicken broth
     1 can (28 ounces) crushed tomatoes
     1 can (16 ounces) kidney beans, rinsed and
        drained
     1 can (15 ounces) garbanzo beans *or*
        chickpeas, rinsed and drained
     1 can (14-1/2 ounces) beef broth
     2 cups frozen cubed hash brown potatoes,
        thawed
     1 tablespoon dried minced onion
     1 tablespoon dried parsley flakes
     1 teaspoon salt
     1 teaspoon dried oregano
  1/2 teaspoon garlic powder
  1/2 teaspoon dried basil
  1/2 teaspoon dried marjoram
     1 package (10 ounces) frozen chopped spinach,
        thawed and drained
     2 cups frozen peas and carrots, thawed

Slow-Cooked Chunky Chili

In a slow cooker, combine the first 13 ingredients. Cover and cook on low for 8 hours. Stir in the spinach, peas and carrots; heat through. **Yield:** 12 servings (about 3 quarts).

Hearty Tomato Pasta Soup

Cook Time: 3-1/2 to 4-1/2 Hours

Lydia Kroese, Minnetonka, Minnesota

I adapted the original recipe for this satisfying soup so I could make it in the slow cooker. It's ideal for staff luncheons at the school where I work, since we don't have easy access to a stove or oven.

     1 pound bulk Italian sausage
     6 cups beef broth
     1 can (28 ounces) stewed tomatoes
     1 can (15 ounces) tomato sauce
     2 cups sliced zucchini
     1 large onion, chopped
     1 cup sliced carrots
     1 cup sliced fresh mushrooms
     1 medium green pepper, chopped
  1/4 cup minced fresh parsley
     2 teaspoons sugar
     1 teaspoon dried oregano
     1 teaspoon dried basil
     1 garlic clove, minced
     2 cups frozen cheese tortellini
Grated Parmesan cheese, optional

In a skillet, cook the sausage over medium heat until no longer pink; drain. Transfer to a 5-qt. slow cooker; add the next 13 ingredients. Cover and cook on high for 3-4 hours or until the vegetables are tender. Cook tortellini according to package directions; drain. Stir into slow cooker; cover and cook 30 minutes longer. Serve with Parmesan cheese if desired. **Yield:** 14 servings (about 3-1/2 quarts).

Savory Cheese Soup

(Pictured below)

Cook Time: 7-1/2 to 8-1/2 Hours

Ann Huseby, Lakeville, Minnesota

This creamy soup is great at parties. Let guests serve themselves and choose from fun garnishes such as popcorn, croutons, green onions and bacon bits.

    3 cans (14-1/2 ounces *each*) chicken broth
    1 small onion, chopped
    1 large carrot, chopped
    1 celery rib, chopped
    1/4 cup chopped sweet red pepper
    2 tablespoons butter *or* margarine
    1 teaspoon salt
    1/2 teaspoon pepper
    1/3 cup all-purpose flour
    1/3 cup cold water
    1 package (8 ounces) cream cheese,
        cubed and softened
    2 cups (8 ounces) shredded cheddar cheese
    1 can (12 ounces) beer, optional
Optional toppings: croutons, popcorn, cooked
    crumbled bacon, sliced green onions

In a slow cooker, combine the first eight ingredients. Cover and cook on low for 7-8 hours. Combine flour and water until smooth; stir into soup. Cover and cook on high 30 minutes longer or until soup is thickened. Stir in cream cheese and cheddar cheese until blended. Stir in beer if desired. Cover and cook on low until heated through. Serve with desired toppings. **Yield:** 6-8 servings.

Savory Cheese Soup

Texas Black Bean Soup

Texas Black Bean Soup

(Pictured above)

Cook Time: 4 to 5 Hours

Pamela Scott, Garland, Texas

This hearty stew made with convenient canned items is perfect for spicing up a family gathering on a cool day. It tastes great and requires so little time and attention.

    2 cans (15 ounces *each*) black beans, rinsed
        and drained
    1 can (14-1/2 ounces) stewed tomatoes *or*
        Mexican stewed tomatoes, cut up
    1 can (14-1/2 ounces) diced tomatoes *or* diced
        tomatoes with green chilies
    1 can (14-1/2 ounces) chicken broth
    1 can (11 ounces) Mexicorn, drained
    2 cans (4 ounces *each*) chopped green chilies
    4 green onions, thinly sliced
    2 to 3 tablespoons chili powder
    1 teaspoon ground cumin
    1/2 teaspoon dried minced garlic

In a slow cooker, combine all ingredients. Cover and cook on high for 4-5 hours or until heated through. **Yield:** 8-10 servings (about 2-1/2 quarts).

Hamburger Vegetable Soup

Cook Time: 8 to 9 Hours

Theresa Jackson, Cicero, New York

I work full-time and have a family of four. We sit down to a home-cooked meal just about every night, many times thanks to my slow cooker. This soup is often on the menu.

1 pound ground beef
1 medium onion, chopped
2 garlic cloves, minced
4 cups V8 juice
1 can (14-1/2 ounces) stewed tomatoes
2 cups coleslaw mix
2 cups frozen green beans
2 cups frozen corn
2 tablespoons Worcestershire sauce
1 teaspoon dried basil
1/2 teaspoon salt
1/4 teaspoon pepper

In a saucepan, cook beef, onion and garlic over medium heat until meat is no longer pink; drain. In a slow cooker, combine the remaining ingredients. Stir in beef mixture. Cover and cook on low for 8-9 hours or until the vegetables are tender. **Yield:** 10 servings.

Pork Chili

(Pictured at right)

Cook Time: 6 Hours

Linda Temple, St. Joseph, Missouri

My husband usually tries to avoid spending time in the kitchen, but he'll frequently offer to prepare this easy chili. Of course, he always eagerly serves as taste tester!

2-1/2 pounds boneless pork, cut into 1-inch cubes
2 tablespoons vegetable oil
1 can (28 ounces) diced tomatoes, undrained
1 can (15-1/2 ounces) chili beans, undrained
1 can (8 ounces) tomato sauce
1/4 cup salsa
1/4 cup chopped onion
1/4 cup chopped green pepper
1 tablespoon chili powder
1 teaspoon minced jalapeno pepper*
1/4 teaspoon garlic powder
1/4 teaspoon cayenne pepper
1/4 teaspoon pepper
1/4 teaspoon salt

In a large skillet over medium-high heat, brown pork in oil; drain. Place in a slow cooker; add remaining ingredients. Cover and cook on high for 2 hours. Reduce heat to low and cook 4 hours longer. **Yield:** 10-12 servings.

*Editor's Note: When cutting or seeing hot peppers, use rubber or plastic gloves to protect your hands. Avoid touching your face.

Faster Slow Cooking

To speed up cooking time on most slow cooker recipes, including soups and stews, follow the general rule that 1 hour on high is equal to 2 hours on low.

Curried Lentil Soup

Cook Time: 8 Hours

Christina Till, South Haven, Michigan

Curry gives a different taste sensation to this chili-like soup. It's delicious with a dollop of sour cream. My family welcomes it with open arms—and watering mouths.

4 cups hot water
1 can (28 ounces) crushed tomatoes
3 medium potatoes, peeled and diced
3 medium carrots, thinly sliced
1 large onion, chopped
1 celery rib, chopped
1 cup lentils
2 garlic cloves, minced
2 bay leaves
4 teaspoons curry powder
1-1/2 teaspoons salt

In a slow cooker, combine all ingredients; stir well. Cover and cook on low for 8 hours or until vegetables and lentils are tender. Discard the bay leaves before serving. **Yield:** 10 servings (2-1/2 quarts).

Pork Chili

Chicken Mushroom Stew

(Pictured below)

Cook Time: 4 Hours

Kim Marie Van Rheenen, Mendota, Illinois

As it simmers, the flavors blend beautifully in this pot of chicken, vegetables and herbs. This stew always draws compliments from those who try it.

- 6 boneless skinless chicken breast halves (1-1/2 pounds)
- 2 tablespoons vegetable oil, *divided*
- 8 ounces fresh mushrooms, sliced
- 1 medium onion, diced
- 3 cups diced zucchini
- 1 cup diced green pepper
- 4 garlic cloves, minced
- 3 medium tomatoes, diced
- 1 can (6 ounces) tomato paste
- 3/4 cup water
- 2 teaspoons salt
- 1 teaspoon *each* dried thyme, oregano, marjoram and basil

Cut chicken into 1-in. cubes; brown in 1 tablespoon oil in a large skillet. Transfer to a slow cooker. In the same skillet, saute the mushrooms, onion, zucchini, green pepper and garlic in remaining oil until crisp-tender. Place in slow cooker. Add tomatoes, tomato paste, water and seasonings. Cover and cook on low for 4 hours or until the vegetables are tender. **Yield:** 6 servings.

Chicken Mushroom Stew

Chicken Stew over Biscuits

Cook Time: 8 to 9 Hours

Kathy Garrett, Browns Mills, New Jersey

A pleasant sauce coats this chicken and veggie dinner that's slow-cooked to tender perfection, then served over biscuits. When I first came up with this dish, my 2-year-old couldn't get enough of it.

- 2 envelopes chicken gravy mix
- 2 cups water
- 3/4 cup white wine *or* chicken broth
- 2 garlic cloves, minced
- 1 tablespoon minced fresh parsley
- 1 to 2 teaspoons chicken bouillon granules
- 1/2 teaspoon pepper
- 5 medium carrots, cut into 1-inch chunks
- 1 large onion, cut into eight wedges
- 1 broiler/fryer chicken (3 to 4 pounds), cut up
- 3 tablespoons all-purpose flour
- 1/3 cup cold water
- 1 tube (7-1/2 ounces) refrigerated buttermilk biscuits

In a slow cooker, combine gravy mix, water, wine or broth, garlic, parsley, bouillon and pepper until blended. Add the carrots, onion and chicken. Cover and cook on low for 7-8 hours. Increase heat to high. In a small bowl, combine the flour and cold water until smooth; gradually stir into slow cooker. Cover and cook for 1 hour. Meanwhile, bake biscuits according to package directions. Place biscuits in soup bowls; top with stew. **Yield:** 4-6 servings.

Green Chili Stew

Cook Time: 7 to 8 Hours

Jacqueline Thompson Graves, Lawrenceville, Georgia

This stew is much heartier than most—and very tasty, too. My family especially enjoys the zippy broth and the generous amounts of tender beef. They frequently request second helpings.

- 2 pounds beef stew meat, cut into 1-inch cubes
- 2 medium onions, chopped
- 2 tablespoons vegetable oil
- 1 can (15 ounces) pinto beans, rinsed and drained
- 1 can (14-1/2 ounces) diced tomatoes, undrained
- 2 cans (4 ounces *each*) chopped green chilies
- 1 cup water
- 3 beef bouillon cubes
- 1 garlic clove, minced
- 1 teaspoon sugar
- 1/2 teaspoon salt
- 1/4 teaspoon pepper
- Shredded cheddar *or* Monterey Jack cheese, optional

In a skillet, brown beef and onions in oil; drain. Transfer to a 5-qt. slow cooker. Combine beans, tomatoes, chilies, water, bouillon, garlic, sugar, salt and pepper; pour over beef. Cover and cook on low for 7-8 hours or until beef is tender. Sprinkle with cheese if desired. **Yield:** 8 servings.

Hobo Meatball Stew

Hobo Meatball Stew

(Pictured above)

Cook Time: 4 to 5 Hours

Margery Bryan, Royal City, Washington

Basic ingredients make this hearty stew a favorite. I usually have everything on hand for this recipe, so it's simple to load up the slow cooker at noon. When I get home, dinner's ready.

- 1 pound ground beef
- 1-1/2 teaspoons salt, *divided*
- 1/2 teaspoon pepper, *divided*
- 4 medium potatoes, peeled and cut into chunks
- 4 medium carrots, cut into chunks
- 1 large onion, cut into chunks
- 1/2 cup ketchup
- 1/2 cup water
- 1-1/2 teaspoons vinegar
- 1/2 teaspoon dried basil

In a bowl, combine beef, 1 teaspoon salt and 1/4 teaspoon pepper; mix well. Shape into 1-in. balls. In a skillet over medium heat, brown meatballs on all sides; drain. Place potatoes, carrots and onion in a slow cooker; top with meatballs. Combine the ketchup, water, vinegar, basil, and remaining salt and pepper; pour over meatballs. Cover and cook on high for 4-5 hours or until the vegetables are tender. **Yield:** 4 servings.

Artichoke Beef Stew

Cook Time: 7-1/2 to 8-1/2 Hours

Janell Schmidt, Athelstane, Wisconsin

The recipe for this special stew was given to me by a dear friend. My family enjoys the deliciously different combination of beef, mushrooms and artichoke hearts.

- 1/3 cup all-purpose flour
- 1 teaspoon salt
- 1/2 teaspoon pepper
- 2-1/2 pounds lean beef stew meat, cut into 1-inch cubes
- 3 tablespoons vegetable oil
- 1 can (10-1/2 ounces) condensed beef consomme, undiluted
- 2 medium onions, halved and sliced
- 1 cup red wine *or* beef broth
- 1 garlic clove, minced
- 1/2 teaspoon dill weed
- 2 jars (6-1/2 ounces *each*) marinated artichoke hearts, drained and chopped
- 20 small fresh mushrooms, halved

Hot cooked noodles

In a shallow bowl or large resealable plastic bag, combine the flour, salt and pepper. Add the beef and toss to coat. In a skillet, brown the beef in oil. Transfer to a slow cooker with a slotted spoon. Gradually add the consomme to the skillet. Bring to a boil; stir to loosen browned bits from pan. Stir in onions, wine or broth, garlic and dill. Pour over beef. Cover and cook on low for 7-8 hours or until the meat is nearly tender.

Stir in the artichokes and mushrooms; cook 30 minutes longer or until heated through. Serve over noodles. **Yield:** 6-8 servings.

Easy Warm Bread

To warm rolls or slices of bread to go with a stew, wrap them in foil and set them in the covered cooker right on top of the hot cooked stew as you're setting the table to serve.

1/3 cup soy sauce
1 to 2 tablespoons chili powder
1 tablespoon dried celery flakes
1/2 teaspoon garlic powder
1/2 teaspoon pepper
1/3 cup cornstarch
1/3 cup cold water
Hot cooked noodles

In a slow cooker, combine the first 10 ingredients. Cover and cook on low for 8 hours. Combine cornstarch and water until smooth; gradually stir into slow cooker. Cover and cook on high for 30 minutes or until slightly thickened. Serve in bowls over noodles. **Yield:** 8-10 servings.

Lots-a-Veggies Stew

Cook Time: 5 Hours

Judy Page, Edenville, Michigan

When I needed a no-fuss meal, I went through my pantry and refrigerator and created this catchall dish.

1 pound ground beef
1 medium onion, diced
2 garlic cloves, minced
1 can (16 ounces) baked beans, undrained
1 can (16 ounces) kidney beans, rinsed and drained
1 can (15 ounces) butter beans, rinsed and drained
1 can (14-1/2 ounces) beef broth
1 can (11 ounces) whole kernel corn, undrained
1 can (10-1/2 ounces) condensed vegetable soup, undiluted
1 can (6 ounces) tomato paste
1 medium green pepper, diced
1 cup sliced carrots
1 cup sliced celery
2 tablespoons chili powder
1 teaspoon dried oregano
1 teaspoon dried thyme
1 teaspoon salt
1/2 teaspoon dried marjoram
1/2 teaspoon pepper

In a skillet, cook beef, onion and garlic over medium heat until meat is no longer pink; drain. Transfer to a 5-qt. slow cooker. Add the remaining ingredients and mix well. Cover and cook on low for 5 hours or until vegetables are tender. **Yield:** 10 servings.

Minestrone Stew

(Pictured above)

Cook Time: 4 to 6 Hours

Janie Hoskins, Red Bluff, California

This stew is made from convenient pantry ingredients, plus it's easy on the pocketbook. You're sure to like the taste.

1 pound ground beef
1 small onion, chopped
1 can (19 ounces) ready-to-serve minestrone soup
1 can (15 ounces) pinto beans, rinsed and drained
1 can (14-1/2 ounces) stewed tomatoes
1 can (11 ounces) whole kernel corn, drained
1 can (4 ounces) chopped green chilies
1 teaspoon salt
1/2 teaspoon garlic powder
1/2 teaspoon onion powder

In a skillet, cook beef and onion until meat is no longer pink; drain. Transfer to a slow cooker. Add the remaining ingredients; mix well. Cover and cook on low for 4-6 hours or until heated through. **Yield:** 8 servings.

Hearty Pork Stew

Cook Time: 8-1/2 Hours

Rebecca Overy, Evanston, Wyoming

Tender chunks of pork combine with colorful tomatoes and green peppers in this spicy, tender stew. I garnish bowls of it with chopped hard-cooked eggs and green onions.

1-1/2 to 2 pounds boneless pork, cut into 1-inch cubes
4 cups water
1 can (14-1/2 ounces) stewed tomatoes
1 medium onion, chopped
1 medium green pepper, chopped

Busy Day Beef Stew

Cook Time: 10 Hours

Beth Wyatt, Paris, Kentucky

I call this my "lazy" stew because it's so easy to make on busy days. It keeps folks coming back for more.

1 boneless beef chuck roast (1 to 1-1/2 pounds)
1 envelope onion soup mix

2 teaspoons browning sauce, optional
1/2 teaspoon salt
1/2 teaspoon pepper
6 cups water
2 cups cubed peeled potatoes (1/2-inch pieces)
6 to 8 medium carrots, cut into chunks
1 medium onion, chopped
1 cup frozen peas, thawed
1 cup frozen corn, thawed
5 tablespoons cornstarch
6 tablespoons cold water

Place roast in a slow cooker; sprinkle with soup mix, browning sauce if desired, salt and pepper. Pour water over meat. Cover and cook on low for 8 hours.

Remove roast to a cutting board; let stand for 5 minutes. Add vegetables to slow cooker. Cube beef and return to slow cooker. Cover and cook on low for 1-1/2 hours or until vegetables are tender. Combine cornstarch and cold water until smooth; stir into stew. Cover and cook on high for 30-45 minutes or until thickened. **Yield:** 8-10 servings.

Apple Chicken Stew

Cook Time: 4 to 5 Hours

Carol Mathias, Lincoln, Nebraska

My husband and I enjoy visiting the apple orchards in nearby Nebraska City. We always buy enough cider to enjoy as a beverage and to use in this sensational slow-cooked stew. It gives this dish a subtle tangy sweetness.

4 medium potatoes, cubed
4 medium carrots, cut into 1/4-inch slices
1 medium red onion, halved and sliced
1 celery rib, thinly sliced
1-1/2 teaspoons salt
3/4 teaspoon dried thyme
1/2 teaspoon pepper
1/4 to 1/2 teaspoon caraway seeds
2 pounds boneless skinless chicken breasts, cubed
2 tablespoons olive *or* vegetable oil
1 large tart apple, peeled and cubed
1-1/4 cups apple cider *or* juice
1 tablespoon cider vinegar
1 bay leaf
Minced fresh parsley

In a slow cooker, layer potatoes, carrots, onion and celery. Combine salt, thyme, pepper and caraway; sprinkle half over vegetables. In a skillet, saute chicken in oil until browned; transfer to slow cooker. Top with apple. Combine apple cider and vinegar; pour over chicken and apple. Sprinkle with remaining salt mixture. Top with bay leaf.

Cover and cook on high for 4-5 hours or until vegetables are tender and chicken juices run clear. Discard bay leaf. Stir before serving. Sprinkle with parsley. **Yield:** 6-8 servings.

Beef Barley Stew

(Pictured below)

Cook Time: 6 to 7 Hours

Barb Smith, Regina, Saskatchewan

On cool days, which we get plenty of here, I like to get out my slow cooker and make up a batch of this comforting stew. Trying to appeal to 10 picky eaters in our large household is not too easy, but with this recipe, everyone asks for seconds.

1-1/2 pounds beef stew meat, cut into 1-inch pieces
1 medium onion, chopped
2 tablespoons vegetable oil
1 quart water
1 can (15 ounces) tomato sauce
5 medium carrots, cut into 1/2-inch pieces
1 celery rib, thinly sliced
2 teaspoons salt
1/2 teaspoon dried oregano
1/2 teaspoon paprika
1/4 teaspoon pepper
2 cups fresh *or* frozen green beans
2 cups fresh *or* frozen corn
3/4 cup medium pearl barley

In a skillet, brown beef and onion in oil; drain. Transfer to a 5-qt. slow cooker. Add water, tomato sauce, carrots, celery, salt, oregano, paprika and pepper. Cover and cook on low for 4-5 hours. Add beans, corn and barley; cover and cook on low 2 hours longer or until barley, beef and vegetables are tender. **Yield:** 6-8 servings.

Beef Barley Stew

Savory Sandwiches

Beef Barbecue

Chapter 3

Barbecued Chicken Sandwiches

from the heat and let stand for 1 hour; drain and rinse. In a large kettle, simmer beans and beef in water for 2 hours or until very tender; drain. Shred beef and place it and the beans in a slow cooker.

In a large skillet, cook bacon until crisp. With a slotted spoon, remove bacon to the slow cooker. Discard all but 3 tablespoons drippings. Saute onion, carrots, celery, peppers and garlic in drippings until tender. Transfer to the slow cooker. Add remaining ingredients except buns. Cover and cook on high for 3-4 hours, stirring often. Remove bay leaf. Spoon 1/2 cup onto each bun. **Yield:** 30 servings.

Barbecued Chicken Sandwiches

(Pictured at left)

Cook Time: 6 to 8 Hours

Roberta Brown, Waupaca, Wisconsin

These sandwiches are great for large gatherings since they have a popular flavor and are convenient to serve. The chicken can be cooked ahead of time, then added to the homemade barbecue sauce for simmering hours before guests arrive.

- 2 broiler-fryer chickens (3 to 3-1/2 pounds *each*), cooked and shredded
- 1 large onion, chopped
- 2 cups water
- 1-1/4 cups ketchup
- 1/4 cup packed brown sugar
- 1/4 cup Worcestershire sauce
- 1/4 cup red wine vinegar *or* cider vinegar
- 1 teaspoon *each* salt, celery seed and chili powder

Favorite Sloppy Joes

Chili Sandwiches

Cook Time: 3 to 4 Hours

Kerry Haglund, Wyoming, Minnesota

No one will be able to resist these special sandwiches stuffed with spicy chili. Of course, the chili also makes a wonderfully filling meal all by itself.

- 1 pound dried navy beans
- 2 pounds beef stew meat
- 2 cups water
- 1 pound sliced bacon, diced
- 1 cup chopped onion
- 1 cup shredded carrots
- 1 cup chopped celery
- 1/3 cup chopped green pepper
- 1/3 cup chopped sweet red pepper
- 4 garlic cloves, minced
- 3 cans (14-1/2 ounces *each*) diced tomatoes, undrained
- 1 cup barbecue sauce
- 1 cup chili sauce
- 1/2 cup honey
- 1/4 cup hot pepper sauce
- 1 tablespoon chili powder
- 1 tablespoon baking cocoa
- 1 tablespoon Dijon mustard
- 1 tablespoon Worcestershire sauce
- 1 bay leaf
- 4 teaspoons beef bouillon granules
- 30 hamburger buns, split

Place the beans and enough water to cover in a saucepan. Bring to a boil; boil for 2 minutes. Remove

1/4 teaspoon hot pepper sauce
Hamburger buns

In a 3-qt. slow cooker, combine all ingredients except buns; mix well. Cook on low for 6-8 hours. Serve on buns. **Yield:** 8-10 servings.

Editor's Note: 6 cups diced cooked chicken may be used instead of the shredded chicken.

Fiesta Pork Sandwiches

Hearty Italian Sandwiches

Cook Time: 6 Hours

Elaine Krupsky, Las Vegas, Nevada

I've been making this sweet and spicy sandwich filling for 35 years. It smells as good as it tastes! It's a great reward for a hungry family after a day working or playing outdoors. It's not uncommon to get requests for second helpings.

  1-1/2 pounds lean ground beef
  1-1/2 pounds bulk Italian sausage
  2 large onions, sliced
  2 large green peppers, sliced
  2 large sweet red peppers, sliced
  1 teaspoon salt
  1 teaspoon pepper
  1/4 teaspoon crushed red pepper flakes
  8 sandwich rolls, split
  Shredded Monterey Jack cheese, optional

In a skillet, brown beef and sausage; drain. Place a third of the onions and peppers in a slow cooker; top with half of the meat mixture. Repeat layers of vegetables and meat, then top with remaining vegetables. Sprinkle with salt, pepper and pepper flakes. Cover and cook on low for 6 hours or until vegetables are tender. With a slotted spoon, serve about 1 cup of meat and vegetables on each roll. Top with cheese if desired. Use pan juices for dipping if desired. **Yield:** 8 servings.

Favorite Sloppy Joes

(Pictured at left)

Cook Time: 6 Hours

Eleanor Mielke, Snohomish, Washington

I've prepared these sandwiches for years. I've tried many sloppy joe recipes, but this one is the best by far. It also travels well for picnics or potlucks.

  2 pounds ground beef
  1/2 cup chopped onion
  3/4 cup chili sauce
  1/2 cup water
  1/4 cup prepared mustard
  2 teaspoons chili powder
  12 hamburger buns, split
  12 slices cheddar cheese

In a large skillet, cook beef and onion over medium heat until meat is no longer pink; drain. Stir in chili sauce, water, mustard and chili powder. Transfer to a slow cooker. Cover and cook on low for 4-6 hours or until flavors are blended. Spoon 1/2 cup onto each bun; top with cheese. **Yield:** 12 servings.

Fiesta Pork Sandwiches

(Pictured above)

Cook Time: 8 to 10 Hours

Yvette Massey, La Luz, New Mexico

This is an easy and flavorful dish that my family really enjoys. When I make these sandwiches for company, I usually prepare the meat the day before, so I can concentrate on side dishes and relaxing with my friends.

  1 boneless pork shoulder roast (3 to 4 pounds)
  1/3 cup lime juice
  2 tablespoons grapefruit juice
  2 tablespoons water
  1 bay leaf
  6 garlic cloves, minced
  1/2 teaspoon salt
  1/2 teaspoon dried oregano
  1/2 teaspoon chili powder
  2 tablespoons olive *or* vegetable oil
  1 large onion, thinly sliced
  12 to 14 sandwich rolls, split

Cut the roast in half; pierce several times with a fork. Place in a large resealable plastic bag or shallow glass container. Combine the next eight ingredients; pour over roast. Cover and refrigerate overnight, turning occasionally. Drain, reserving marinade. In a skillet over medium heat, brown the roast in oil on all sides. Place onion, roast and marinade in a slow cooker. Cover and cook on high for 2 hours.

Reduce heat to low; cook 6-8 hours longer or until the meat is tender. Remove roast; shred or thinly slice. Discard the bay leaf. Skim fat from cooking juices and transfer to a saucepan; bring to a rolling boil. Serve pork on rolls with juices as a dipping sauce. **Yield:** 12-14 servings.

Savory Beef Sandwiches

(Pictured below)

Cook Time: 6 to 8 Hours

Lynn Williamson, Hayward, Wisconsin

Before heading to work in the morning, I'll get this going in the slow cooker. Then it's all ready to serve as soon as my husband and I walk in.

> 1 tablespoon dried minced onion
> 2 teaspoons salt
> 2 teaspoons garlic powder
> 2 teaspoons dried oregano
> 1 teaspoon dried rosemary, crushed
> 1 teaspoon caraway seeds
> 1 teaspoon dried marjoram
> 1 teaspoon celery seed
> 1/4 teaspoon cayenne pepper
> 1 boneless chuck roast (3 to 4 pounds), halved
> 8 to 10 sandwich rolls, split

Combine seasonings; rub over roast. Place in a slow cooker. Cover and cook on low for 6-8 hours or until meat is tender. Shred with a fork. Serve on rolls. **Yield:** 8-10 servings.

Editor's Note: No liquid is added to the slow cooker. The moisture comes from the roast.

Pork and Beef Barbecue

Cook Time: 6 to 8 Hours

Corbin Detgen, Buchanan, Michigan

My wife, Dixie, and I love to share sandwiches made with this tender meaty filling simmered in a zippy sauce.

> 1 can (6 ounces) tomato paste
> 1/2 cup packed brown sugar
> 1/4 cup chili powder

Savory Beef Sandwiches

Italian Turkey Sandwiches

> 1/4 cup cider vinegar
> 2 teaspoons Worcestershire sauce
> 1 teaspoon salt
> 1-1/2 pounds beef stew meat, cut into 3/4-inch cubes
> 1-1/2 pounds pork chop suey meat *or* pork tenderloin, cut into 3/4-inch cubes
> 3 green peppers, chopped
> 2 large onions, chopped
> 14 sandwich rolls, split

Lettuce and tomatoes, optional

In a slow cooker, combine the first six ingredients. Stir in beef, pork, green peppers and onions. Cover and cook on high for 6-8 hours or until meat is tender. Shred meat with two forks. Serve on rolls with lettuce and chopped tomatoes if desired. **Yield:** 14 servings.

Italian Turkey Sandwiches

(Pictured above)

Cook Time: 5 to 6 Hours

Carol Riley, Galva, Illinois

I hope you enjoy these tasty turkey sandwiches as much as our family does. The recipe makes plenty, so it's great for potlucks. Leftovers are just as good reheated the next day.

> 1 bone-in turkey breast (5-1/2 pounds), skin removed
> 1/2 cup chopped green pepper
> 1 medium onion, chopped
> 1/4 cup chili sauce
> 3 tablespoons white vinegar
> 2 tablespoons dried oregano *or* Italian seasoning

4 teaspoons beef bouillon granules
11 kaiser *or* hard sandwich rolls, split

Place the turkey breast, green pepper and onion in a 5-qt. slow cooker coated with nonstick cooking spray. Combine the chili sauce, vinegar, oregano and bouillon; pour over turkey and vegetables. Cover and cook on low for 5-6 hours or until meat juices run clear and vegetables are tender. Remove turkey with a slotted spoon, reserving cooking liquid. Shred the turkey with two forks; return to cooking juices. Spoon 1/2 cup onto each roll. **Yield:** 11 servings.

Savory Chicken Sandwiches

Cook Time: 8 to 9 Hours

Joan Parker, Gastonia, North Carolina

With eight children under 12, I know how to make family-pleasing meals. This tender chicken tastes like you fussed, but requires few ingredients. You can also thicken the juices and serve it over rice.

   4 bone-in chicken breast halves
   4 chicken thighs
   1 envelope onion soup mix
   1/4 teaspoon garlic salt
   1/4 cup prepared Italian salad dressing
   1/4 cup water
   14 to 16 hamburger buns, split

Remove skin from chicken if desired. Place chicken in a 5-qt. slow cooker. Sprinkle with soup mix and garlic salt. Pour dressing and water over chicken. Cover and cook on low for 8-9 hours. Remove chicken; cool slightly. Skim fat from cooking juices. Remove chicken from bones; cut into bite-size pieces and return to slow cooker. Serve with a slotted spoon on buns. **Yield:** 14-16 servings.

Shredded French Dip

(Pictured below)

Cook Time: 6 to 8 Hours

Carla Kimball, Callaway, Nebraska

This chuck roast, slow-simmered in a beefy broth, is delicious when shredded and spooned onto rolls. Serve the cooking juices in individual cups for dipping.

   1 boneless beef chuck roast (3 pounds), trimmed
   1 can (10-1/2 ounces) condensed French onion soup, undiluted
   1 can (10-1/2 ounces) condensed beef consomme, undiluted
   1 can (10-1/2 ounces) condensed beef broth, undiluted
   1 teaspoon beef bouillon granules
   8 to 10 French *or* Italian rolls, split

Halve roast and place in a slow cooker. Combine the soup, consomme, broth and bouillon; pour over roast. Cover and cook on low for 6-8 hours or until meat is tender. Remove meat and shred with two forks. Serve on rolls. Skim fat from cooking juices and serve as a dipping sauce. **Yield:** 8-10 servings.

Shredded French Dip

Hot Ham Sandwiches

Hot Ham Sandwiches

(Pictured above)

Cook Time: 4 to 5 Hours

Susan Rehm, Grahamsville, New York

I came up with this crowd-pleasing recipe when trying to re-create a favorite sandwich from a restaurant near my hometown. Flavored with sweet relish, these ham sandwiches are oh-so-easy. My family likes them with coleslaw and French fries.

  3 pounds thinly sliced deli ham
  (about 40 slices)
  2 cups apple juice
  2/3 cup packed brown sugar
  1/2 cup sweet pickle relish
  2 teaspoons prepared mustard
  1 teaspoon paprika
 12 kaiser rolls, split
Additional sweet pickle relish, optional

Separate ham slices and place in a slow cooker. In a bowl, combine the apple juice, brown sugar, relish, mustard and paprika. Pour over ham. Cover and cook on low for 4-5 hours or until heated through. Place 3-4 slices of ham on each roll. Serve with additional relish if desired. **Yield: 12 servings.**

Thawing Required

Frozen meat should be completely thawed before placing in a slow cooker. Whole roasts and poultry should be cut in half or into smaller pieces to ensure thorough cooking.

Italian Meatball Subs

Cook Time: 4 to 5 Hours

Jean Glacken, Elkton, Maryland

This is one of those recipes you always come back to. A flavorful tomato sauce and mildly spiced meatballs make a hearty sandwich filling, or they can be served over pasta. I broil the meatballs first to quickly brown them.

  2 eggs, beaten
  1/4 cup milk
  1/2 cup dry bread crumbs
  2 tablespoons grated Parmesan cheese
  1 teaspoon salt
  1/4 teaspoon pepper
  1/8 teaspoon garlic powder
  1 pound ground beef
  1/2 pound bulk Italian sausage
SAUCE:
  1 can (15 ounces) tomato sauce
  1 can (6 ounces) tomato paste
  1 small onion, chopped
  1/2 cup chopped green pepper
  1/2 cup red wine *or* beef broth
  1/3 cup water
  2 garlic cloves, minced
  1 teaspoon dried oregano
  1 teaspoon salt
  1/2 teaspoon sugar
  1/2 teaspoon pepper
  6 to 7 Italian rolls, split
Additional Parmesan cheese, optional

In a bowl, combine eggs and milk; add bread crumbs, Parmesan cheese, salt, pepper and garlic powder. Add beef and sausage; mix well. Shape into 1-in. balls. Broil 4 in. from the heat for 4 minutes; turn and broil 3 minutes longer. Transfer to a slow cooker.

  Combine tomato sauce and paste, onion, green pepper, wine or broth, water and seasonings; pour over meatballs. Cover and cook on low for 4-5 hours. Serve on rolls. Sprinkle with cheese if desired. **Yield: 6-7 servings.**

Italian Venison Sandwiches

Cook Time: 8 Hours

Andrew Henson, Morrison, Illinois

The slow cooker makes easy work of these hearty venison sandwiches. The meat always comes out tender and tasty. That makes it a favorite for an avid hunter and cook like me.

  2 cups water
  1 envelope onion soup mix
  1 tablespoon dried basil
  1 tablespoon dried parsley flakes
  1 teaspoon beef bouillon granules
  1/2 teaspoon celery salt
  1/4 teaspoon garlic powder
  1/4 teaspoon cayenne pepper
  1/4 teaspoon pepper
  1 boneless venison roast (3 to 4 pounds), cut
  into 1-inch cubes

Tangy Barbecue Sandwiches

Shred meat and return to sauce; heat through. Use a slotted spoon to serve on buns. **Yield:** 14-18 servings.

Herbed French Dip Sandwiches

Cook Time: 10 to 12 Hours

Dianne Joy Richardson, Colorado Springs, Colorado

(Pictured below)

I found this recipe in one of our local publications. It's great for an easy meal any time of year, since the meat cooks all day without any attention.

>   1 lean beef roast (3 to 4 pounds)
> 1/2 cup soy sauce
>   1 beef bouillon cube
>   1 bay leaf
>   3 to 4 whole peppercorns
>   1 teaspoon dried rosemary, crushed
>   1 teaspoon dried thyme
>   1 teaspoon garlic powder
> Hard rolls *or* French bread

Remove and discard all visible fat from roast. Place in a slow cooker. Combine soy sauce, bouillon and spices; pour over roast. Add water to almost cover roast. Cover and cook over low heat for 10-12 hours or until meat is very tender.

Remove meat; reserve cooking juices. Shred meat with two forks. Serve on hard rolls or French bread slices. Serve cooking juices as a dipping sauce. **Yield:** 12 servings.

10 to 12 sandwich rolls, split
Green pepper rings, optional

In a slow cooker, combine the first nine ingredients. Add venison and stir. Cover and cook on low for 8 hours or until meat is tender. Using a slotted spoon, spoon into rolls. Top with pepper rings if desired. **Yield:** 10-12 servings.

Tangy Barbecue Sandwiches

(Pictured above)

Cook Time: 7 to 8 Hours

Debbi Smith, Crossett, Arkansas

Since I prepare the beef for these robust sandwiches in the slow cooker, it's easy to fix a meal for a hungry bunch. The savory homemade sauce assures I come home with no leftovers from potluck dinners and other gatherings.

>   3 cups chopped celery
>   1 cup chopped onion
>   1 cup ketchup
>   1 cup barbecue sauce
>   1 cup water
>   2 tablespoons vinegar
>   2 tablespoons Worcestershire sauce
>   2 tablespoons brown sugar
>   1 teaspoon chili powder
>   1 teaspoon salt
> 1/2 teaspoon pepper
> 1/2 teaspoon garlic powder
>   1 boneless chuck roast (3 to 4 pounds),
>   trimmed
>   14 to 18 hamburger buns, split

In a slow cooker, combine the first 12 ingredients; mix well. Add roast. Cover and cook on high for 7-8 hours or until meat is tender. Remove roast; cool.

Herbed French Dip Sandwiches

Teriyaki Sandwiches

(Pictured below)

Cook Time: 7 to 9 Hours

Bernice Muilenburg, Molalla, Oregon

The meat for these sandwiches comes out of the slow cooker tender and flavorful. Living as we do in the foothills of the Cascades, we frequently have venison and elk in the freezer. I sometimes substitute that in this recipe, and it never tastes like game.

    2 pounds boneless chuck steak
    1/4 cup soy sauce
    1 tablespoon brown sugar
    1 teaspoon ground ginger
    1 garlic clove, minced
    4 teaspoons cornstarch
    2 tablespoons water
    8 French rolls, split
    1/4 cup butter *or* margarine, melted
Pineapple rings
Chopped green onions

Cut steak into thin slices. In a slow cooker, combine soy sauce, sugar, ginger and garlic. Add steak. Cover and cook on low for 7-9 hours or until meat is tender. Remove meat with a slotted spoon; set aside.

Carefully pour liquid into a 2-cup measuring cup; skim fat. Add water to liquid to measure 1-1/2 cups. Pour into a large saucepan. Combine cornstarch and water until smooth; add to pan. Cook and stir until thick and bubbly, about 2 minutes. Add meat and heat through. Brush rolls with butter; broil 4-5 in. from the heat for 2-3 minutes or until lightly toasted. Fill with meat, pineapple and green onions. **Yield:** 8 servings.

Dilly Beef Sandwiches

Cook Time: 8 to 9 Hours

Donna Blankenheim, Madison, Wisconsin

My younger sister, Jean, shared this recipe, which puts a twist on the traditional barbecue sandwich. As a busy mother of four, Jean never has much time to cook, but she does like to entertain. This crowd-pleaser, which takes mere minutes of prep time, is perfect for our large family gatherings.

    1 boneless beef chuck roast (3 to 4 pounds)
    1 jar (16 ounces) whole dill pickles, undrained
    1/2 cup chili sauce
    2 garlic cloves, minced
    10 to 12 hamburger buns, split

Cut roast in half and place in a slow cooker. Add pickles with juice, chili sauce and garlic. Cover and cook on low for 8-9 hours or until beef is tender. Discard pickles. Remove roast. When cool enough to handle, shred the meat. Return to the sauce and heat through. Using a slotted spoon, fill each bun with about 1/2 cup meat mixture. **Yield:** 10-12 servings.

Italian Beef Hoagies

Cook Time: 8 Hours

Lori Piatt, Danville, Illinois

You'll need just five ingredients to feed a crowd these tender tangy sandwiches. On weekends, I start the roast the night before, so I can shred it in the morning.

    1 boneless sirloin tip roast (about 4 pounds), halved
    2 envelopes Italian salad dressing mix

Teriyaki Sandwiches

Meat Loaf Burgers

juice, garlic, ketchup, bay leaf, Italian seasoning and remaining salt. Pour over the patties. Cover and cook on low for 7-9 hours or until meat is tender. Discard bay leaf. Separate patties with a spatula if necessary; serve on buns. **Yield:** 6 servings.

Beef Barbecue

(Pictured below and on page 34)

Cook Time: 6 to 8 Hours

Karen Walker, Sterling, Virginia

We like to keep our freezer stocked with plenty of beef roasts. When we're not in the mood for pot roast, I prepare these satisfying sandwiches instead. The meat cooks in a tasty sauce while I'm away at work. Then I just slice it thinly and serve it on rolls. These sandwiches are hard to beat.

    1 boneless chuck roast (3 pounds)
    1 cup barbecue sauce
  1/2 cup apricot preserves
  1/3 cup chopped green *or* sweet red pepper
    1 small onion, chopped
    1 tablespoon Dijon mustard
    2 teaspoons brown sugar
  12 sandwich rolls, split

Cut the roast into quarters; place in a greased 5-qt. slow cooker. In a bowl, combine barbecue sauce, preserves, green pepper, onion, mustard and brown sugar; pour over roast. Cover and cook on low for 6-8 hours or until meat is tender.

Remove roast and thinly slice; return meat to slow cooker and stir gently. Cover and cook 20-30 minutes longer. Skim fat from sauce. Serve beef and sauce on rolls. **Yield:** 12 servings.

    2 cups water
    1 jar (16 ounces) mild pepper rings, undrained
  18 hoagie buns, split

Place roast in a 5-qt. slow cooker. Combine the salad dressing mix and water; pour over roast. Cover and cook on low for 8 hours or until meat is tender. Remove meat; shred with a fork and return to slow cooker. Add pepper rings; heat through. Spoon 1/2 cup meat mixture onto each bun. **Yield:** 18 servings.

Meat Loaf Burgers

(Pictured above)

Cook Time: 7 to 9 Hours

Peggy Burdick, Burlington, Michigan

These hearty sandwiches are great for potluck dinners. Served on hamburger buns, the beefy patties get extra flavor when topped with the seasoned tomato sauce. People love them since they're a fun change from plain burgers and regular meat loaf.

    1 large onion, sliced
    1 celery rib, chopped
    2 pounds lean ground beef
1-1/2 teaspoons salt, *divided*
  1/4 teaspoon pepper
    2 cups tomato juice
    4 garlic cloves, minced
    1 tablespoon ketchup
    1 bay leaf
    1 teaspoon Italian seasoning
    6 hamburger buns, split

Place onion and celery in a slow cooker. Combine beef, 1 teaspoon salt and pepper; shape into six patties. Place over onion mixture. Combine tomato

Beef Barbecue

Beef & Ground Beef

Slow-Cooked Pepper Steak (p. 50)

Chapter 4

Slow Cooker Enchiladas

1 cup (4 ounces) shredded Monterey Jack cheese
6 flour tortillas (6 or 7 inches)

In a skillet, cook beef, onion and green pepper until beef is no longer pink and vegetables are tender; drain. Add the next eight ingredients; bring to a boil. Reduce heat; cover and simmer for 10 minutes. Combine cheeses. In a 5-qt. slow cooker, layer about 3/4 cup beef mixture, one tortilla and about 1/3 cup cheese. Repeat layers. Cover and cook on low for 5-7 hours or until heated through. **Yield:** 4 servings.

Beef in Mushroom Gravy

Cook Time: 7 to 8 Hours

Margery Bryan, Royal City, Washington

This is one of the best and easiest meals I've ever made. It has only four ingredients, and they all go into the pot at once. The meat is nicely seasoned and makes its own gravy—it tastes wonderful when you serve it over mashed potatoes.

    2 to 2-1/2 pounds boneless round steak
    1 to 2 envelopes dry onion soup mix
    1 can (10-3/4 ounces) condensed cream of
       mushroom soup, undiluted
  1/2 cup water
Mashed potatoes, optional

Cut steak into six serving-size pieces; place in a 3-qt. slow cooker. Combine soup mix, soup and water; pour over beef. Cover and cook on low for 7-8 hours or until meat is tender. Serve with mashed potatoes if desired. **Yield:** 6 servings.

Beefy Au Gratin Potatoes

Cook Time: 4 Hours

Eileen Majerus, Pine Island, Minnesota

It's easy to vary the flavor of this hearty family-favorite casserole by using different kinds of soup and potato mixes. We enjoy the comforting combination of beef, potatoes and vegetables in this dish. I usually serve up heaping helpings with a salad and garlic bread.

    1 package (5-1/4 ounces) au gratin or cheddar
      and bacon potatoes

It's Best to Brown

For the best color and flavor, ground beef should be browned before using it in a slow cooker recipe. The exception is when preparing a meat loaf or similar dish.

Although it's not necessary to brown other cuts of meat or poultry, the process can enhance the flavor and appearance and reduce the fat in the finished dish.

Slow Cooker Enchiladas

(Pictured above)

Cook Time: 5 to 7 Hours

Mary Luebbert, Benton, Kansas

As a busy wife and mother of two young sons, I rely on this handy recipe. I layer enchilada ingredients in the slow cooker, turn it on and forget about it. With a bit of spice, these hearty enchiladas are especially nice during the colder months.

    1 pound ground beef
    1 cup chopped onion
  1/2 cup chopped green pepper
    1 can (16 ounces) pinto or kidney beans, rinsed
      and drained
    1 can (15 ounces) black beans, rinsed and
      drained
    1 can (10 ounces) diced tomatoes and green
      chilies, undrained
  1/3 cup water
    1 teaspoon chili powder
  1/2 teaspoon ground cumin
  1/2 teaspoon salt
  1/4 teaspoon pepper
    1 cup (4 ounces) shredded sharp
      cheddar cheese

1 can (15-1/4 ounces) whole kernel corn,
   drained
1 can (10-3/4 ounces) condensed cream of
   potato soup, undiluted
1 cup water
1 can (4 ounces) chopped green chilies,
   drained
1 can (4 ounces) mushroom stems and pieces,
   drained
1 jar (4 ounces) diced pimientos, drained
1 pound ground beef
1 medium onion, chopped

Set potato sauce mix aside. Place potatoes in a slow cooker; top with corn. In a bowl, combine soup, water, chilies, mushrooms, pimientos and reserved sauce mix; mix well. Pour a third of the mixture over corn.

In a skillet, cook beef and onion over medium heat until the meat is no longer pink; drain. Transfer to slow cooker. Top with remaining sauce mixture. Do not stir. Cover and cook on low for 4 hours or until potatoes are tender. **Yield:** 4-6 servings.

Beef and Barley

Cook Time: 4 Hours

Linda Ronk, Melbourne, Florida

I like to double this country-style dish to serve company. I'm not sure where the recipe originated, but I've served it with pleasure for many years.

2 pounds ground beef, cooked and drained
1 can (15 ounces) diced carrots, undrained
1 can (14-1/2 ounces) diced tomatoes,
   undrained
1 can (10-3/4 ounces) condensed tomato soup,
   undiluted
2 celery ribs, finely chopped
1/2 cup water
1-1/2 to 2 teaspoons salt
1/2 teaspoon pepper
1/2 teaspoon chili powder
1 teaspoon Worcestershire sauce
1 bay leaf
1 cup quick-cooking barley
2 tablespoons butter *or* margarine
1 cup soft bread crumbs
1 cup (4 ounces) shredded cheddar cheese

In a slow cooker, combine the first 11 ingredients. In a skillet, lightly brown barley in butter. Add to the slow cooker; mix well. Sprinkle with bread crumbs and cheese. Cover and cook on high for 4 hours or until heated through. Discard bay leaf before serving. **Yield:** 8 servings.

Slow Cooker Lasagna

(Pictured below)

Cook Time: 4 to 5 Hours

Lisa Micheletti, Collierville, Tennessee

Convenient no-cook lasagna noodles take the work out of this traditional favorite adapted for the slow cooker. Because it's so easy to assemble, it's great for work days as well as weekends. We like it accompanied by garlic bread or Parmesan cheese toast.

1 pound ground beef
1 large onion, chopped
2 garlic cloves, minced
1 can (29 ounces) tomato sauce
1 cup water
1 can (6 ounces) tomato paste
1 teaspoon salt
1 teaspoon dried oregano
1 package (8 ounces) no-cook lasagna noodles
4 cups (16 ounces) shredded mozzarella cheese
1-1/2 cups (12 ounces) small-curd cottage cheese
1/2 cup grated Parmesan cheese

In a skillet, cook beef, onion and garlic over medium heat until meat is no longer pink; drain. Add the tomato sauce, water, tomato paste, salt and oregano; mix well. Spread a fourth of the meat sauce in an ungreased 5-qt. slow cooker. Arrange a third of the noodles over sauce (break noodles if necessary).

Combine the cheeses; spoon a third of the mixture over noodles. Repeat layers twice. Top with remaining meat sauce. Cover and cook on low for 4-5 hours or until noodles are tender. **Yield:** 6-8 servings.

Slow Cooker Lasagna

Stuffed Flank Steak

Saucy Italian Roast

Cook Time: 8 to 9 Hours

Jan Roat, Grass Range, Montana

This tender roast is one of my favorite fix-it-and-forget-it meals. I thicken the juices with a little flour and add ketchup, then serve the sauce and beef slices over pasta. It's a deliciously different Italian-style main dish.

>   1 boneless rump roast (3 to 3-1/2 pounds)
>   1/2 to 1 teaspoon salt
>   1/2 teaspoon garlic powder
>   1/4 teaspoon pepper
>   1 jar (4-1/2 ounces) sliced mushrooms, drained
>   1 medium onion, diced
>   1 jar (14 ounces) spaghetti sauce
>   1/4 to 1/2 cup red wine *or* beef broth
> Hot cooked pasta

Cut the roast in half. Combine salt, garlic powder and pepper; rub over roast. Place in a 5-qt. slow cooker. Top with mushrooms and onion. Combine the spaghetti sauce and wine or broth; pour over meat and vegetables. Cover and cook on low for 8-9 hours or until meat is tender. Slice roast; serve over pasta with pan juices. **Yield:** 8-10 servings.

Pepper Beef Goulash

Cook Time: 4 to 5 Hours

Peggy Key, Grant, Alabama

I use only a couple of common ingredients to turn beef stew meat into a hearty entree. No one will ever guess the secret behind this great goulash—an envelope of sloppy joe seasoning.

>   1/2 cup water
>   1 can (6 ounces) tomato paste

>   2 tablespoons cider vinegar
>   1 envelope sloppy joe seasoning
>   2 to 2-1/4 pounds beef stew meat
>   (3/4-inch cubes)
>   1 celery rib, cut into 1/2-inch slices
>   1 medium green pepper, cut into 1/2-inch
>   chunks
> Hot cooked noodles

In a 3-qt. slow cooker, combine the water, tomato paste, vinegar and sloppy joe seasoning. Stir in the beef, celery and green pepper. Cover and cook on high for 4-5 hours. Serve over noodles. **Yield:** 4-5 servings.

Stuffed Flank Steak

(Pictured above)

Cook Time: 6 to 8 Hours

Diane Hixon, Niceville, Florida

This elegant meal is worthy of company. The tender steak cuts easily into appetizing spirals for serving, and extra stuffing cooks conveniently in a foil packet on top of the steak.

>   1 package (8 ounces) crushed corn bread
>   stuffing
>   1 cup chopped onion
>   1 cup chopped celery
>   1/4 cup minced fresh parsley
>   2 eggs
> 1-1/4 cups beef broth
>   1/3 cup butter *or* margarine, melted
>   1/2 teaspoon seasoned salt
>   1/2 teaspoon pepper
> 1-1/2 pounds flank steak

In a large bowl, combine stuffing, onion, celery and parsley. In a small bowl, beat the eggs; stir in broth and butter. Pour over stuffing mixture. Sprinkle with seasoned salt and pepper; stir well. Pound steak to 1/2-in. thickness. Spread 1-1/2 cups stuffing mixture over steak. Roll up, starting with a short side; tie with string.

Place in a 5-qt. slow cooker. Remaining stuffing can be wrapped tightly in foil and placed over the rolled steak. Cover and cook on low for 6-8 hours or until a meat thermometer inserted in stuffing reads 165°. Remove string before slicing. **Yield:** 6 servings.

Editor's Note: No liquid is added to the slow cooker. The moisture comes from the meat.

Hearty New England Dinner
(Pictured below right)

Cook Time: 7-1/2 to 9-1/2 Hours

Claire McCombs, San Diego, California

This favorite slow-cooker recipe came from a friend. At first, my husband was a bit skeptical about a roast that wasn't fixed in the oven, but he loves the old-fashioned goodness of this version. The horseradish in the gravy adds zip.

  2 medium carrots, sliced
  1 medium onion, sliced
  1 celery rib, sliced
  1 boneless chuck roast (about 3 pounds)
  1 teaspoon salt, *divided*
1/4 teaspoon pepper
  1 envelope onion soup mix
  2 cups water
  1 tablespoon vinegar
  1 bay leaf
1/2 small head cabbage, cut into wedges
  3 tablespoons butter *or* margarine
  2 tablespoons all-purpose flour
  1 tablespoon dried minced onion
  2 tablespoons prepared horseradish

Place carrots, onion and celery in a 5-qt. slow cooker. Place the roast on top; sprinkle with 1/2 teaspoon salt and pepper. Add soup mix, water, vinegar and bay leaf. Cover and cook on low for 7-9 hours or until beef is tender. Remove beef and keep warm; discard bay leaf. Add cabbage. Cover and cook on high for 30-40 minutes or until cabbage is tender.

Meanwhile, melt butter in a small saucepan; stir in flour and onion. Add 1-1/2 cups cooking liquid from the slow cooker. Stir in horseradish and remaining salt; bring to a boil. Cook and stir over low heat until thick and smooth, about 2 minutes. Serve with roast and vegetables. **Yield:** 6-8 servings.

Try to Trim Down

When preparing meat or poultry for the slow cooker, trim off excess fat. It retains heat, and large amounts of fat could raise the temperature of the cooking liquid, causing the meat to overcook.

Garlic Beef Stroganoff
Cook Time: 7 to 8 Hours

Erika Anderson, Wausau, Wisconsin

I'm a mom and work full-time, so I try to use my slow cooker whenever possible. This Stroganoff is perfect because I can get it ready in the morning before the kids get up.

  2 teaspoons beef bouillon granules
  1 cup boiling water
  1 can (10-3/4 ounces) condensed
    cream of mushroom soup, undiluted
  2 jars (4-1/2 ounces *each*) sliced mushrooms,
    drained
  1 large onion, chopped
  3 garlic cloves, minced
  1 tablespoon Worcestershire sauce
1-1/2 to 2 pounds boneless round steak, trimmed
    and cut into thin strips
  2 tablespoons vegetable oil
  1 package (8 ounces) cream cheese, cubed
Hot cooked noodles

In a slow cooker, dissolve bouillon in water. Add soup, mushrooms, onion, garlic and Worcestershire sauce. In a skillet, brown beef in oil. Transfer to the slow cooker. Cover and cook on low for 7-8 hours or until the meat is tender. Stir in cream cheese until smooth. Serve over noodles. **Yield:** 6-8 servings.

Hearty New England Dinner

Slow-Cooked Pepper Steak

Slow-Cooked Pepper Steak

(Pictured above and on page 44)

Cook Time: 6 to 7 Hours

Sue Gronholz, Columbus, Wisconsin

After a long day in our greenhouse raising bedding plants for sale, I appreciate coming in to this hearty beef dish for supper.

1-1/2 to 2 pounds beef round steak
   2 tablespoons vegetable oil
 1/4 cup soy sauce
   1 cup chopped onion
   1 garlic clove, minced
   1 teaspoon sugar
 1/2 teaspoon salt
 1/4 teaspoon pepper
 1/4 teaspoon ground ginger
   4 tomatoes, cut into eighths *or* 1 can
     (14-1/2 ounces) diced tomatoes, undrained
   2 large green peppers, cut into strips
 1/2 cup cold water
   1 tablespoon cornstarch
Hot cooked noodles *or* rice

Cut beef into 3-in. x 1-in. strips; brown in oil in a skillet. Transfer to a slow cooker. Combine the next seven ingredients; pour over beef. Cover and cook on low for 5-6 hours or until meat is tender. Add tomatoes and green peppers; cook on low for 1 hour longer. Combine the cold water and cornstarch to make a paste; stir into liquid in slow cooker and cook on high until thickened. Serve over noodles or rice. **Yield:** 6-8 servings.

Crock Pot Pizza

Cook Time: 3 to 4 Hours

Julie Sterchi, Harrisburg, Illinois

Always a hit at our church dinners, this hearty casserole keeps folks coming back for more.

   1 package (16 ounces) wide egg noodles
1-1/2 pounds ground beef *or* turkey
 1/4 cup chopped onion
   1 jar (26 ounces) spaghetti sauce
   1 jar (4-1/2 ounces) sliced mushrooms, drained
1-1/2 teaspoons Italian seasoning
   1 package (3-1/2 ounces) sliced pepperoni, halved
   3 cups (12 ounces) shredded mozzarella cheese
   3 cups (12 ounces) shredded cheddar cheese

Cook noodles according to package directions. Meanwhile, in a large skillet, cook beef and onion over medium heat until meat is no longer pink; drain. Stir in spaghetti sauce, mushrooms and Italian seasoning. Drain noodles.

In a 5-qt. slow cooker coated with nonstick cooking spray, spread a third of the meat sauce. Cover with a third of the noodles and pepperoni. Sprinkle with a third of the cheeses. Repeat layers twice. Cover and cook on low for 3-4 hours or until heated through and cheese is melted. **Yield:** 6-8 servings.

Steak 'n' Gravy

Cook Time: 8-1/2 Hours

Betty Janway, Ruston, Louisiana

Served over rice or mashed potatoes, this nicely spiced steak makes a satisfying meal. I like how tender economical round steak is when it comes out of the slow cooker.

- **1 pound round steak, trimmed**
- **1 tablespoon vegetable oil**
- **1-1/2 cups water**
- **1 can (8 ounces) tomato sauce**
- **1 teaspoon ground cumin**
- **1 teaspoon garlic powder**
- **1/2 teaspoon salt**
- **1/4 teaspoon pepper**
- **2 tablespoons all-purpose flour**
- **1/4 cup cold water**
- **Hot cooked rice *or* mashed potatoes**

Cut the beef into bite-size pieces; brown in oil in a skillet. Transfer to a slow cooker. Cover with water; add the tomato sauce and seasonings. Cover and cook on low for 8 hours or until meat is tender.

In a small bowl, combine the flour and cold water to make a paste; stir into liquid in the slow cooker. Cover and cook on high 30 minutes longer or until the gravy is thickened. Serve over rice or potatoes. **Yield:** 4 servings.

Slow-Cooked Tamale Casserole

(Pictured at right)

Cook Time: 4 Hours

Diana Briggs, Veneta, Oregon

I've been making this recipe for years because my family really likes it. It's great for busy days, since you assemble it earlier in the day and let it cook.

- **1 pound ground beef**
- **1 egg**
- **1-1/2 cups milk**
- **3/4 cup cornmeal**
- **1 can (15-1/4 ounces) whole kernel corn, drained**
- **1 can (14-1/2 ounces) diced tomatoes, undrained**
- **1 can (2-1/4 ounces) sliced ripe olives, drained**
- **1 envelope chili seasoning**
- **1 teaspoon seasoned salt**
- **1 cup (4 ounces) shredded cheddar cheese**

In a skillet, cook beef over medium heat until no longer pink; drain. In a bowl, combine the egg, milk and cornmeal until smooth. Add corn, tomatoes, olives, chili seasoning, seasoned salt and beef. Transfer to a greased slow cooker. Cover and cook on

high for 3 hours and 45 minutes. Sprinkle with cheese; cover and cook 15 minutes longer or until cheese is melted. **Yield:** 6 servings.

Flank Steak Roll-Up

Cook Time: 8 to 10 Hours

Sheryl Johnson, Las Vegas, Nevada

As a working mother of five hungry boys, I rely on my slow cooker to give me a head start on meals. For this special yet filling dish, I roll stuffing mix and mushrooms into flank steak before simmering it in an easy gravy.

- **1 can (4 ounces) mushroom stems and pieces, undrained**
- **2 tablespoons butter *or* margarine, melted**
- **1 package (6 ounces) seasoned stuffing mix**
- **1 beef flank steak (1-3/4 pounds)**
- **1 envelope brown gravy mix**
- **1/4 cup chopped green onions**
- **1/4 cup dry red wine *or* beef broth**

In a bowl, toss the mushrooms, butter and dry stuffing mix. Spread over steak to within 1 in. of edges. Roll up jelly-roll style, starting with a long side; tie with kitchen string. Place in a slow cooker. Prepare gravy mix according to package directions; add onions and wine or broth. Pour over meat. Cover and cook on low for 8-10 hours.

Remove meat to a serving platter and keep warm. Strain cooking juices and thicken if desired. Remove string from roll-up; slice and serve with gravy. **Yield:** 6 servings.

Slow-Cooked Tamale Casserole

Smoky Beef 'n' Beans

Cook Time: 6 to 7 Hours

Anita Curtis, Camarillo, California

Liquid smoke gives a unique taste to this thick and hearty combination of beef and beans. I serve it with a crisp salad to make a complete meal.

    1 pound ground beef
    1 cup chopped onion
   12 bacon strips, cooked and crumbled
    2 cans (16 ounces *each*) pork and beans
    1 can (16 ounces) kidney beans, rinsed and
       drained
    1 can (16 ounces) butter beans, drained
    1 cup ketchup
  1/4 cup packed brown sugar
    3 tablespoons vinegar
    1 teaspoon liquid smoke, optional
  1/2 teaspoon salt
  1/4 teaspoon pepper

In a skillet, cook the beef and onion until meat is no longer pink; drain. Transfer to a slow cooker. Stir in the remaining ingredients. Cover and cook on low for 6-7 hours or until heated through. **Yield:** 8 servings.

Slow-Cooked Swiss Steak

(Pictured below)

Cook Time: 8 to 9 Hours

Kathie Morris, Redmond, Oregon

This recipe originally came from my mom and I changed it a bit to suit my family. Everyone raves about how tender and rich-tasting this dish is. Even our two young kids love it. Leftovers

Why Pay More?

Economical, less tender cuts of beef like round steak, stew meat and cube steak are perfect for the slow cooker. The long, slow cooking process achieved with the use of this handy appliance ensures fork-tender, moist and flavorful meat even on cuts that would be tough and chewy prepared using other cooking methods.

from a double batch make super Stroganoff the next night. I crumble the meat and mix it with the gravy, plus sour cream and Worcestershire sauce.

  3/4 cup all-purpose flour
    1 teaspoon pepper
  1/4 teaspoon salt
    2 to 2-1/2 pounds boneless round steak
    1 to 2 tablespoons butter *or* margarine
    1 can (10-3/4 ounces) condensed cream of
       mushroom soup, undiluted
1-1/3 cups water
    1 cup sliced celery, optional
  1/2 cup chopped onion
    1 garlic clove, minced
    1 to 3 teaspoons beef bouillon granules

In a shallow bowl, combine flour, pepper and salt. Cut steak into six serving-size pieces; dredge in flour mixture. In a skillet, brown steak in butter. Transfer to a slow cooker. Combine the remaining ingredients; pour over steak. Cover and cook on low for 8-9 hours or until the meat is tender. **Yield:** 6 servings.

Slow-Cooked Swiss Steak

Beef & Ground Beef

Slow-Cooked Short Ribs

(Pictured at right)

Cook Time: 9 to 10 Hours

Pam Halfhill, Medina, Ohio

Smothered in a mouth-watering barbecue sauce, these meaty ribs are a popular entree wherever I serve them. The recipe is great for a busy cook—after everything is combined, the slow cooker does all the work.

2/3 cup all-purpose flour
2 teaspoons salt
1/2 teaspoon pepper
4 to 4-1/2 pounds boneless beef short ribs
1/4 to 1/3 cup butter *or* margarine
1 large onion, chopped
1-1/2 cups beef broth
3/4 cup red wine vinegar *or* cider vinegar
3/4 cup packed brown sugar
1/2 cup chili sauce
1/3 cup ketchup
1/3 cup Worcestershire sauce
5 garlic cloves, minced
1-1/2 teaspoons chili powder

In a large resealable plastic bag, combine the flour, salt and pepper. Add ribs in batches and shake to coat. In a large skillet, brown ribs in butter. Transfer to a 5-qt. slow cooker. In the same skillet, combine the remaining ingredients. Cook and stir until mixture comes to a boil; pour over ribs (slow cooker will be full). Cover and cook on low for 9-10 hours or until meat is tender. **Yield:** 12-15 servings.

Slow-Cooked Short Ribs

Corned Beef and Cabbage

Cook Time: 8 to 9 Hours

Karen Waters, Laurel, Maryland

I first tried this fuss-free way to cook traditional corned beef and cabbage for St. Patrick's Day a few years ago. Now it's a regular in my menu planning. This is terrific with Dijon mustard and crusty bread.

1 medium onion, cut into wedges
4 medium potatoes, peeled and quartered
1 pound baby carrots
3 cups water
3 garlic cloves, minced
1 bay leaf
2 tablespoons sugar
2 tablespoons cider vinegar
1/2 teaspoon pepper
1 corned beef brisket with spice packet (2-1/2 to 3 pounds), cut in half
1 small head cabbage, cut into wedges

Place the onion, potatoes and carrots in a 5-qt. slow cooker. Combine water, garlic, bay leaf, sugar, vinegar, pepper and contents of spice packet; pour over vegetables. Top with brisket and cabbage. Cover and cook on low for 8-9 hours or until meat and vegetables are tender. Remove bay leaf before serving. **Yield:** 6-8 servings.

Sweet-Sour Beef

Cook Time: 7 to 8 Hours

Beth Husband, Billings, Montana

Pasta lovers will savor this sweet and sour specialty over noodles. Chock-full of tender beef, sliced carrots, green pepper and onion, this stew-like sauce is also a hit over rice. This is a great change-of-pace supper.

2 pounds boneless round *or* chuck steak, cut into 1-inch cubes
2 tablespoons vegetable oil
2 cans (8 ounces *each*) tomato sauce
2 cups sliced carrots
2 cups pearl onions
1 large green pepper, cut into 1-inch pieces
1/2 cup molasses
1/3 cup vinegar
1/4 cup sugar
2 teaspoons chili powder
2 teaspoons paprika
1 teaspoon salt
Shell macaroni and snipped chives, optional

In a skillet, brown steak in oil; transfer to a 5-qt. slow cooker. Add the next 10 ingredients; stir well. Cover and cook on low for 7-8 hours or until meat is tender. Thicken if desired. Serve over macaroni and garnish with chives if desired. **Yield:** 10-12 servings.

Italian Bow Tie Supper

Cook Time: 7 to 8 Hours

Joy Frey, Kelso, Missouri

I appreciate the convenience of this hearty Italian meal. Its delicious flavor reminds me of ravioli—but it's so much less fuss. The recipe makes a lot, so I don't have to cook on the night we enjoy the leftovers.

1-1/2 pounds ground beef
  1 medium onion, chopped
  1 garlic clove, minced
  2 cans (8 ounces *each*) tomato sauce
  1 can (14-1/2 ounces) stewed tomatoes, cut up
  1 teaspoon dried oregano
  1 teaspoon Italian seasoning
Salt and pepper to taste
  1 package (16 ounces) bow tie pasta, cooked and drained
  1 package (10 ounces) frozen chopped spinach, thawed and well drained
1-1/2 cups (6 ounces) shredded mozzarella cheese
  1/2 cup grated Parmesan cheese

In a skillet, cook beef, onion and garlic over medium heat until meat is no longer pink; drain. Transfer to a slow cooker. Stir in the tomato sauce, tomatoes and seasonings. Cover and cook on low for 7-8 hours or until bubbly.

Increase heat to high; stir in pasta, spinach and cheeses. Cover and cook for 10 minutes or until heated through and the cheese is melted. **Yield:** 6 servings.

Steak Burritos

Cook Time: 8 to 9 Hours

Valerie Jones, Portland, Maine

I spice up flank steak with convenient taco seasoning packets. Slowly simmered all day, the beef is tender and a snap to shred. Just fill flour tortillas and add toppings for a tasty, time-easing Southwestern meal.

  2 flank steaks (about 1 pound *each*)
  2 envelopes taco seasoning
  1 medium onion, chopped
  1 can (4 ounces) chopped green chilies
  1 tablespoon vinegar
 10 flour tortillas (7 inches)
1-1/2 cups (6 ounces) shredded Monterey Jack cheese
1-1/2 cups chopped seeded plum tomatoes
  3/4 cup sour cream

Cut steaks in half; rub with taco seasoning. Place in a slow cooker coated with nonstick cooking spray. Top with onion, chilies and vinegar. Cover and cook on low for 8-9 hours or until meat is tender. Remove the steaks and cool slightly; shred the meat with two forks.

Return to slow cooker; heat through. Spoon about 1/2 cup meat mixture down the center of each tortilla. Top with cheese, tomato and sour cream. Fold ends and sides over filling. **Yield:** 10 servings.

How to Shred Meat

For the best results when shredding meat, follow this method:

Remove the cooked meat from the slow cooker, with a slotted spoon if necessary. Reserve the cooking liquid if called for. Place the meat in a shallow pan or platter. With two forks, pull the meat into thin shreds. Return the shredded meat to the slow cooker to warm or use as the recipe directs.

Slow-Cooked Coffee Pot Roast

Cook Time: 9-1/2 to 10-1/2 Hours

Janet Dominick, Bagley, Minnesota

As a working wife and mother of three, I don't have much time to fix meals. I spend a few minutes in the morning putting together this entree, and it tastes like I spent hours at it.

  2 medium onions, thinly sliced
  2 garlic cloves, minced
  1 boneless beef chuck roast
    (3-1/2 to 4 pounds), quartered
  1 cup brewed coffee
1/4 cup soy sauce
1/4 cup cornstarch
  6 tablespoons cold water

Place half of the onions in a 5-qt. slow cooker. Top with garlic and half of the beef. Top with remaining onion and beef. Combine coffee and soy sauce; pour over beef. Cover and cook on low for 9-10 hours or until meat is tender. Combine cornstarch and water until smooth; stir into cooking juices. Cover and cook on high for 30 minutes or until gravy is thickened. **Yield:** 10-12 servings.

Meal-in-One Casserole

Cook Time: 4 Hours

Dorothy Pritchett, Wills Point, Texas

Salsa gives zip to this hearty no-fuss meal. This recipe makes more than my husband and I can eat, so I freeze half of it. We think it tastes even better the second time.

  1 pound ground beef
  1 medium onion, chopped
  1 medium green pepper, chopped
  1 can (15-1/4 ounces) whole kernel corn, drained
  1 can (4 ounces) mushroom stems and pieces, drained
  1 teaspoon salt
1/4 teaspoon pepper

1 jar (11 ounces) salsa
5 cups cooked medium egg noodles
1 can (28 ounces) diced tomatoes, undrained
1 cup (4 ounces) shredded cheddar cheese *or*
    blend of cheddar, Monterey Jack and
    American cheeses

In a skillet, cook beef and onion over medium heat until meat is no longer pink; drain. Transfer to a slow cooker. Top with the green pepper, corn and mushrooms. Sprinkle with salt and pepper. Pour salsa over mushrooms. Top with noodles. Pour tomatoes over all. Sprinkle with cheese. Cover and cook on low for 4 hours or until heated through. **Yield:** 4-6 servings.

Slow-Cooked Meat Loaf

(Pictured below)

Cook Time: 8 to 9 Hours

Marna Heitz, Farley, Iowa

What could be more comforting to come home to than moist and tender homemade meat loaf? This one retains its shape in the slow cooker and slices beautifully. Because the potatoes and carrots cook along with the meat loaf, the entire dinner is ready at the same time.

1 egg
1/4 cup milk
2 slices day-old bread, cubed
1/4 cup finely chopped onion
2 tablespoons finely chopped green pepper
1 teaspoon salt
1/4 teaspoon pepper
1-1/2 pounds lean ground beef
1/4 cup ketchup
8 medium carrots, cut into 1-inch chunks
8 small red potatoes

In a bowl, beat egg and milk. Stir in the bread cubes, onion, green pepper, salt and pepper. Add the beef and mix well. Shape into a round loaf. Place in a 5-qt. slow cooker. Spread ketchup on top of loaf. Arrange carrots around loaf. Peel a strip around the center of each potato; place potatoes over carrots. Cover and cook on high for 1 hour. Reduce heat to low; cover and cook 7-8 hours longer or until meat is no longer pink and the vegetables are tender. **Yield:** 4 servings.

Slow-Cooked Meat Loaf

Slow-Cooked Rump Roast

Combine cornstarch and cold water until smooth; stir into slow cooker. Cover and cook on high for 30 minutes or until gravy is thickened. **Yield:** 6-8 servings.

Stuffed Cabbage Casserole

Cook Time: 4 to 5 Hours

Joann Alexander, Center, Texas

I came up with this recipe because I love the taste of cabbage rolls but don't always have the time to prepare them. My version uses the same ingredients in a simpler manner for hearty results everyone enjoys!

- 1 pound ground beef
- 1 small onion, chopped
- 4 cups chopped cabbage
- 1 medium green pepper, chopped
- 1 cup uncooked instant rice
- 1 cup water
- 1 can (6 ounces) tomato paste
- 1 can (14-1/2 ounces) diced tomatoes, undrained
- 1/2 cup ketchup
- 2 tablespoons vinegar
- 1 to 2 tablespoons sugar, optional
- 1 tablespoon Worcestershire sauce
- 1-1/2 teaspoons salt
- 1/2 teaspoon pepper
- 1/4 teaspoon garlic powder

In a skillet, cook the beef and onion over medium heat until the meat is no longer pink; drain. Transfer to a slow cooker; add the cabbage, green pepper and rice. In a bowl, combine the water and tomato paste. Stir in the remaining ingredients. Pour over the beef mixture; mix well. Cover and cook on low for 4-5 hours or until the rice and vegetables are tender. **Yield:** 4-6 servings.

Slow-Cooked Rump Roast

(Pictured above)

Cook Time: 10-1/2 to 11-1/2 Hours

Mimi Walker, Palmyra, Pennsylvania

Cooking pot roast in horseradish sauce in the slow cooker is a tasty new twist. It gives a tangy flavor, tender vegetables and great gravy that even my 6- and 3-year-olds love.

- 1 boneless beef rump roast (3 to 3-1/2 pounds)
- 2 tablespoons vegetable oil
- 4 medium carrots, halved lengthwise and cut into 2-inch pieces
- 3 medium potatoes, peeled and cut into chunks
- 2 small onions, sliced
- 1/2 cup water
- 6 to 8 tablespoons horseradish sauce
- 1/4 cup red wine vinegar *or* cider vinegar
- 1/4 cup Worcestershire sauce
- 2 garlic cloves, minced
- 1-1/2 to 2 teaspoons celery salt
- 3 tablespoons cornstarch
- 1/3 cup cold water

Cut roast in half. In a large skillet, brown meat on all sides in oil over medium-high heat; drain. Place carrots and potatoes in a 5-qt. slow cooker. Top with meat and onions. Combine the water, horseradish sauce, vinegar, Worcestershire sauce, garlic and celery salt. Pour over meat. Cover and cook on low for 10-11 hours or until meat and vegetables are tender.

Mushroom Beef and Noodles

Cook Time: 8 Hours

Virgil Killman, Mascoutah, Illinois

I've prepared this flavorful beef dish many times for family and friends. I've also shared the easy six-ingredient recipe with lots of cooks, and everyone thinks it's great. People taste this dish and think I worked a lot harder on it.

- 1 can (10-3/4 ounces) condensed golden mushroom soup, undiluted
- 1 can (10-3/4 ounces) condensed beefy mushroom soup, undiluted
- 1 can (10-3/4 ounces) condensed French onion soup, undiluted
- 1/4 cup seasoned bread crumbs
- 2 pounds beef stew meat, cut into 1/2-inch cubes
- 1 package (12 ounces) wide egg noodles

In a slow cooker, combine soups and bread crumbs; mix well. Stir in beef. Cover and cook on low for 8 hours or until meat is tender. Cook noodles according to package directions; drain. Serve with beef mixture. **Yield:** 6-8 servings.

Cube Steaks with Gravy

(Pictured below)

Cook Time: 8-1/2 Hours

Judy Long, Limestone, Tennessee

With this recipe, good flavor doesn't take a back seat to convenience. Cube steaks can be tough and chewy. But fixed this way, they're a tender and tasty family favorite.

- **1/3 cup all-purpose flour**
- **6 beef cube steaks (1-1/2 pounds)**
- **1 tablespoon vegetable oil**
- **1 large onion, sliced and separated into rings**
- **3 cups water, *divided***
- **1 envelope brown gravy mix**
- **1 envelope mushroom gravy mix**
- **1 envelope onion gravy mix**
- **Hot mashed potatoes *or* cooked noodles**

Place flour in a large resealable plastic bag. Add steaks, a few at a time, and shake until completely coated. In a skillet, cook steaks in oil until lightly browned on each side. Transfer to a slow cooker. Add the onion and 2 cups water. Cover and cook on low for 8 hours or until meat is tender.

In a bowl, whisk together gravy mixes with remaining water. Add to slow cooker; cook 30 minutes longer. Serve over mashed potatoes or noodles. **Yield:** 6 servings.

Slow-Cooked Flank Steak

Cook Time: 7 to 8 Hours

Michelle Armistead, Keyport, New Jersey

My slow cooker gets lots of use, especially during the hectic summer months. I can prepare this savory flank steak in the morning and then completely forget about it until dinnertime. I serve it with noodles and a tossed salad. This easy meal wins raves from those who try it.

- **1 flank steak (about 1-1/2 pounds), cut in half**
- **1 tablespoon vegetable oil**
- **1 large onion, sliced**
- **1/3 cup water**
- **1 can (4 ounces) chopped green chilies**
- **2 tablespoons vinegar**
- **1-1/4 teaspoons chili powder**
- **1 teaspoon garlic powder**
- **1/2 teaspoon sugar**
- **1/2 teaspoon salt**
- **1/8 teaspoon pepper**

In a skillet, brown the steak in oil; transfer to a slow cooker. In the same skillet, saute the onion for 1 minute. Gradually add the water, stirring to loosen browned bits from pan. Add remaining ingredients; bring to a boil. Pour over the flank steak. Cover and cook on low for 7-8 hours or until the meat is tender. Slice the meat; serve with onion and pan juices. **Yield:** 4-6 servings.

Cube Steaks with Gravy

Beef and Beans

Cook Time: 6-1/2 to 8-1/2 Hours

Marie Leadmon, Bethesda, Maryland

This deliciously spicy steak and beans over rice will have family and friends asking for more. It's a favorite in my recipe collection because it's so simple and so good.

- **1-1/2 pounds boneless round steak**
- **1 tablespoon prepared mustard**
- **1 tablespoon chili powder**
- **1/2 teaspoon salt**
- **1/4 teaspoon pepper**
- **1 garlic clove, minced**
- **2 cans (14-1/2 ounces *each*) diced tomatoes, undrained**
- **1 medium onion, chopped**
- **1 beef bouillon cube, crushed**
- **1 can (16 ounces) kidney beans, rinsed and drained**
- **Hot cooked rice**

Cut steak into thin strips. Combine mustard, chili powder, salt, pepper and garlic in a bowl; add steak and toss to coat. Transfer to a slow cooker; add tomatoes, onion and bouillon. Cover and cook on low for 6-8 hours. Stir in beans; cook 30 minutes longer. Serve over rice. **Yield:** 8 servings.

Gone-All-Day Casserole

Cook Time: 6 to 8 Hours

Janet Haak Aarness, Pelican Rapids, Minnesota

Even less expensive cuts of meat become wonderfully tender when cooked slowly in this savory casserole. Wild rice and almonds give this meal a special look and taste.

- **1 cup uncooked wild rice, rinsed and drained**
- **1 cup chopped celery**
- **1 cup chopped carrots**
- **2 cans (4 ounces *each*) mushroom stems and pieces, drained**
- **1 large onion, chopped**
- **1 garlic clove, minced**
- **1/2 cup slivered almonds**
- **3 beef bouillon cubes**
- **2-1/2 teaspoons seasoned salt**
- **2 pounds boneless round steak, cut into 1-inch cubes**
- **3 cups water**

Place ingredients in order listed in a slow cooker (do not stir). Cover and cook on low for 6-8 hours or until rice is tender. Stir before serving. **Yield:** 12 servings.

Spread It Out

For meats to cook evenly in the slow cooker, allow some space between the pieces, so the heat can circulate and the seasonings can be nicely distributed.

Chili Mac

(Pictured below)

Cook Time: 6 Hours

Marie Posavec, Berwyn, Illinois

This recipe has appeared on my menus once a month for more than 40 years...it's never failed to please. I've also turned it into a soup by adding a can of beef broth.

- **1 pound ground beef, cooked and drained**
- **2 cans (15 ounces *each*) hot chili beans, undrained**
- **2 large green peppers, chopped**
- **1 large onion, chopped**
- **4 celery ribs, chopped**
- **1 can (8 ounces) tomato sauce**
- **1 envelope chili seasoning**
- **2 garlic cloves, minced**
- **1 package (7 ounces) elbow macaroni, cooked and drained**
- **Salt and pepper to taste**

In a slow cooker, combine the first eight ingredients; mix well. Cover and cook on low for 6 hours or until heated through. Stir in macaroni; mix well. Season with salt and pepper. **Yield:** 12 servings.

Chili Mac

Meaty Spaghetti Sauce

Meaty Spaghetti Sauce

(Pictured above)

Cook Time: 8 Hours

Arlene Sommers, Redmond, Washington

My family always enjoyed my homemade spaghetti sauce, but it's so time-consuming to make on the stovetop. My busy grown daughter adapted my recipe to take advantage of her slow cooker. The flavorful sauce still receives compliments.

> 1 pound ground beef
> 1 pound bulk Italian sausage
> 1 medium green pepper, chopped
> 1 medium onion, chopped
> 8 garlic cloves, minced
> 3 cans (14-1/2 ounces *each*) Italian diced tomatoes, drained
> 2 cans (15 ounces *each*) tomato sauce
> 2 cans (6 ounces *each*) tomato paste
> 1/3 cup sugar
> 2 tablespoons Italian seasoning
> 1 tablespoon dried basil
> 2 teaspoons dried marjoram
> 1 teaspoon salt
> 1/2 teaspoon pepper

Hot cooked spaghetti

In a large skillet over medium heat, cook beef and sausage until no longer pink; drain. Transfer to a 5-qt. slow cooker. Stir in green pepper, onion, garlic, tomatoes, tomato sauce, paste, sugar and seasonings; mix well. Cover and cook on low for 8 hours or until bubbly. Serve over spaghetti. **Yield:** 12 servings.

Taco Meat Loaf

Cook Time: 8 Hours

Diane Essinger, Findlay, Ohio

Our children think there are three basic food groups—pizza, tacos and burgers! They like to doctor up slices of this specially seasoned meat loaf with their favorite taco toppings. It's a tasty meal we all enjoy.

> 1 egg
> 1/2 cup sour cream
> 1/3 cup salsa
> 2 to 4 tablespoons taco seasoning
> 1 cup crushed tortilla chips
> 1/2 cup shredded cheddar cheese
> 2 pounds lean ground beef

Optional toppings: sour cream, salsa, shredded cheddar cheese, shredded lettuce, sliced ripe olives

In a large bowl, combine the first six ingredients. Crumble beef over mixture and mix well. Pat into the bottom of a slow cooker. Cover and cook on low for 8 hours or until a meat thermometer reads 160°. Top with sour cream, salsa, cheese, lettuce and olives if desired. **Yield:** 8 servings.

Chicken & Turkey

Herbed Chicken and Veggies (p. 68)

Chapter 5

Cranberry Chicken

(Pictured below)

Cook Time: 5-1/2 to 6-1/2 Hours

Sandy Brooks, Tacoma, Washington

Cooking with cranberries is a happy habit for me. I like to include them because the fruit is filled with vitamin C—and my husband and son love the flavor. This chicken recipe is the one they request the most.

    1 cup fresh *or* frozen cranberries
3/4 cup chopped onion
1/2 teaspoon salt
1/4 teaspoon ground cinnamon
1/4 teaspoon ground ginger
    1 broiler/fryer chicken (about 3-1/2 pounds), quartered and skin removed
    1 cup orange juice
    1 teaspoon grated orange peel
    3 tablespoons butter *or* margarine, melted
    3 tablespoons all-purpose flour
    2 to 3 tablespoons brown sugar
Hot cooked noodles

In a slow cooker, combine first five ingredients; top with chicken. Pour orange juice over chicken and sprinkle with orange peel. Cover and cook on low for 5-6 hours or until meat juices run clear. Remove chicken; debone and cut up meat. Set aside and keep warm.

    Combine butter and flour until smooth; add to slow cooker. Cook on high until thickened, about 20 minutes. Stir in chicken and brown sugar; heat through. Serve over noodles. **Yield:** 4-6 servings.

Speed Up Prep Time

Slow cooker recipes sometimes call for a broiler/fryer chicken that is quartered or cut into pieces and skinned. You can save yourself additional preparation time by asking the butcher to cut up and skin the chicken for you.

Turkey in Cream Sauce

Cook Time: 7 to 8 Hours

Kathy-Jo Winterbottom, Pottstown, Pennsylvania

I've been relying on this recipe for tender turkey since I first moved out on my own years ago. I serve it whenever I invite new guests to the house, and I'm constantly sharing the recipe.

1-1/4 cups white wine *or* chicken broth
    1 medium onion, chopped
    2 garlic cloves, minced
    2 bay leaves
    2 teaspoons dried rosemary, crushed
1/2 teaspoon pepper
    3 turkey breast tenderloins (3/4 pound *each*)
    3 tablespoons cornstarch
1/2 cup half-and-half cream *or* milk
1/2 teaspoon salt

In a slow cooker, combine wine or broth, onion, garlic and bay leaves. Combine rosemary and pep-

Cranberry Chicken

Fruited Chicken

Cover and cook on low for 7-8 hours or until chicken juices run clear. Serve over rice. **Yield:** 6 servings.

No-Fuss Chicken
(Pictured below)

Cook Time: 2 to 2-1/2 Hours

Sandra Flick, Toledo, Ohio

My mother-in-law devised this recipe when her children were growing up and schedules were hectic. It was a favorite Sunday dish because it could be cooking while the family was at church. When they came home, it didn't take long to finish the preparations and put dinner on the table.

> 2/3 cup all-purpose flour
> 1 teaspoon dried sage
> 1 teaspoon dried basil
> 1 teaspoon seasoned salt
> 1 broiler/fryer chicken (2-1/2 to 3 pounds), cut up
> 1/4 cup butter *or* margarine
> 2 cups chicken broth

In a shallow bowl, combine flour, sage, basil and seasoned salt; coat chicken. Reserve remaining flour mixture. In a large skillet, melt butter; brown chicken on all sides. Transfer to a slow cooker. Add 1/4 cup reserved flour mixture to the skillet (discarding the rest); stir until smooth. When mixture begins to bubble, stir in chicken broth and bring to a boil; boil for 1 minute. Pour over chicken. Cover and cook on high for 2 to 2-1/2 hours or until chicken juices run clear. **Yield:** 4 servings.

per; rub over turkey. Place in slow cooker. Cover and cook on low for 7-8 hours or until meat is tender. Remove turkey and keep warm. Strain cooking juices; pour into a saucepan.

Combine cornstarch, cream and salt until smooth; gradually add to juices. Bring to a boil; cook and stir for 2 minutes or until thickened and bubbly. Slice turkey; serve with cream sauce. **Yield:** 9 servings.

Fruited Chicken
(Pictured above)

Cook Time: 7 to 8 Hours

Mirien Church, Aurora, Colorado

With three young children, I appreciate the ease of preparing entrees like this with my slow cooker. The combination of fruity flavors in this chicken dish is unique and tasty. My husband loves having hot home-cooked meals each night…and this particular one is always a hit!

> 1 large onion, sliced
> 6 boneless skinless chicken breast halves
> 1/3 cup orange juice
> 2 tablespoons soy sauce
> 2 tablespoons Worcestershire sauce
> 2 tablespoons Dijon mustard
> 1 tablespoon grated orange peel
> 2 garlic cloves, minced
> 1/2 cup chopped dried apricots
> 1/2 cup dried cranberries
> Hot cooked rice

Place onion and chicken in a 5-qt. slow cooker. Combine the orange juice, soy sauce, Worcestershire sauce, mustard, orange peel and garlic; pour over chicken. Sprinkle with apricots and cranberries.

No-Fuss Chicken

Chicken in a Pot

Cook Time: 7 to 9 Hours

Alpha Wilson, Roswell, New Mexico

It takes just minutes to get this satisfying supper ready for the slow cooker. And at the end of a busy day, your family will appreciate the simple goodness of tender chicken and vegetables. It's one of our favorite meals.

> 3 medium carrots, cut into 3/4-inch pieces
> 2 celery ribs with leaves, cut into 3/4-inch pieces
> 2 medium onions, sliced
> 1 broiler/fryer chicken (3 to 4 pounds), cut up
> 1/2 cup chicken broth
> 1-1/2 teaspoons salt
> 1 teaspoon dried basil
> 1/2 teaspoon pepper

In a 5-qt. slow cooker, place carrots, celery and onions. Top with chicken. Combine remaining ingredients; pour over chicken. Cover and cook on low for 7-9 hours or until chicken juices run clear and vegetables are tender. Serve with a slotted spoon. **Yield:** 6 servings.

Stuffed Sweet Peppers

(Pictured below)

Cook Time: 4 to 5 Hours

Judy Earl, Sarasota, Florida

Italian sausage gives zest to the rice filling in these tender peppers, which I have prepared often over the years. When I married in 1970, slow cookers were the rage. In our home, it's one appliance that's never gone out of style.

> 3 medium sweet red peppers
> 2 medium sweet yellow peppers
> 1 jar (14 ounces) spaghetti sauce, *divided*
> 3/4 pound uncooked bulk Italian turkey sausage
> 3/4 cup uncooked instant rice
> 1/2 cup crumbled feta *or* blue cheese
> 1/2 cup chopped onion
> 1/4 cup chopped tomato
> 1/4 cup minced fresh parsley
> 2 tablespoons sliced ripe olives
> 1/4 to 1/2 teaspoon garlic powder
> 1/2 teaspoon salt
> 1/2 teaspoon Italian seasoning
> 1/2 teaspoon crushed red pepper flakes

Cut tops off peppers; chop tops and set aside. Discard stems and seeds; set pepper cups aside. Reserve 3/4 cup spaghetti sauce; pour the remaining sauce into a slow cooker. Combine the sausage, rice, cheese, onion, tomato, parsley, olives, garlic powder, salt, Italian seasoning, red pepper flakes and reserved chopped peppers and spaghetti sauce.

Spoon into pepper cups; place in slow cooker. Cover and cook on low for 4-5 hours or until peppers are tender. **Yield:** 5 servings.

Golden Chicken and Noodles

Cook Time: 6 to 7 Hours

Charlotte McDaniel, Anniston, Alabama

This tender chicken cooks up in a golden sauce that is nicely flavored with basil. It's great for taking to a potluck supper, especially if you work and don't have time to cook during the day. Classic flavors make it very popular on the buffet.

> 6 boneless skinless chicken breast halves (1-1/2 pounds)
> 2 cans (10-3/4 ounces *each*) condensed broccoli cheese soup, undiluted
> 2 cups milk
> 1 small onion, chopped
> 1/2 to 1 teaspoon salt
> 1/2 to 1 teaspoon dried basil
> 1/8 teaspoon pepper
> Hot cooked noodles

Cut chicken pieces in half; place in a 5-qt. slow cooker. Combine the soup, milk, onion, salt, basil and pepper; pour over chicken. Cover and cook on high

Stuffed Sweet Peppers

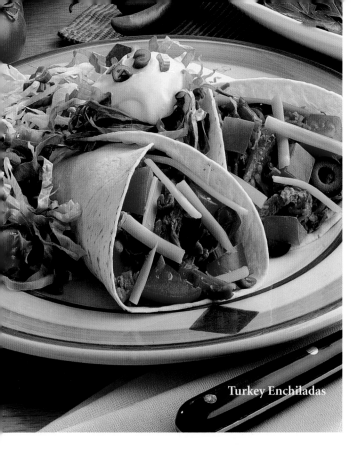

Turkey Enchiladas

the filling and roll up. Add the toppings of your choice. **Yield:** 4 servings.

Slow-Cooked Orange Chicken

(Pictured below)

Cook Time: 4-1/2 Hours

Nancy Wit, Fremont, Nebraska

Everyone who tries this saucy chicken likes the taste, including my grandchildren. A hint of orange gives the chicken a delicious flavor. It travels well, and I often take it to potluck suppers.

    1 broiler/fryer chicken (3 pounds), cut up
      and skin removed
    3 cups orange juice
    1 cup chopped celery
    1 cup chopped green pepper
    1 can (4 ounces) mushroom stems and
      pieces, drained
    4 teaspoons dried minced onion
    1 tablespoon minced fresh parsley
      or 1 teaspoon dried parsley flakes
  1/2 teaspoon salt
  1/4 teaspoon pepper
    3 tablespoons cornstarch
    3 tablespoons cold water
Hot cooked rice, optional

Combine the first nine ingredients in a slow cooker. Cover and cook on low for 4 hours or until meat juices run clear. Combine cornstarch and water until smooth; stir into cooking juices. Cover and cook on high for 30-45 minutes or until thickened. Serve over rice if desired. **Yield:** 4 servings.

for 1 hour. Reduce heat to low; cover and cook 5-6 hours longer or until the meat juices run clear. Serve over noodles. **Yield:** 6 servings.

Turkey Enchiladas

(Pictured above)

Cook Time: 6 to 8 Hours

Stella Schams, Tempe, Arizona

I was pleased to discover a different way to serve an economical cut of meat. I simmer turkey thighs with tomato sauce, green chilies and seasonings until they're tender and flavorful. Then I shred the turkey and serve it in tortillas with other fresh fixings.

    2 turkey thighs *or* drumsticks (about 2 pounds)
    1 can (8 ounces) tomato sauce
    1 can (4 ounces) chopped green chilies
  1/3 cup chopped onion
    2 tablespoons Worcestershire sauce
    1 to 2 tablespoons chili powder
  1/4 teaspoon garlic powder
    8 flour tortillas (6 inches)
Optional toppings: chopped green onions, sliced
    ripe olives, chopped tomatoes, shredded cheddar
    cheese, sour cream *and/or* shredded lettuce

Remove skin from the turkey. Place in a 5-qt. slow cooker. Combine the tomato sauce, chilies, onion, Worcestershire sauce, chili powder and garlic powder; pour over turkey. Cover and cook on low for 6-8 hours or until the turkey is tender.

Remove the turkey; shred the meat with a fork and return to the slow cooker. Heat through. Spoon about 1/2 cup of the turkey mixture down the center of each tortilla. Fold bottom of the tortilla over

Slow-Cooked Orange Chicken

Chicken a la King

Slow Cooker Chicken Dinner

Cook Time: 8-1/2 Hours

Jenet Cattar, Neptune Beach, Florida

I love using my slow cooker because it's so convenient. This meal-in-one, which includes juicy chicken and tasty veggies in a creamy sauce, is ready to eat when I get home from the office. It's great to walk in the door and smell this cooking.

6 medium red potatoes, cut into chunks
4 medium carrots, cut into 1/2-inch pieces
4 boneless skinless chicken breast halves
1 can (10-3/4 ounces) condensed cream of chicken soup, undiluted
1 can (10-3/4 ounces) condensed cream of mushroom soup, undiluted
1/8 teaspoon garlic salt
2 to 4 tablespoons mashed potato flakes, optional

Place potatoes and carrots in a slow cooker. Top with chicken. Combine the soups and garlic salt; pour over chicken. Cover and cook on low for 8 hours. To thicken if desired, stir potato flakes into the gravy and cook 30 minutes longer. **Yield:** 4 servings.

Chicken a la King

(Pictured above)

Cook Time: 7-1/2 to 8-1/2 Hours

Eleanor Mielke, Snohomish, Washington

When I know I'll be having a busy day with little time for cooking, I prepare this tasty main dish. Brimming with tender chick-en and colorful vegetables, it has a tempting aroma while cook-ing—and tastes even better.

1 can (10-3/4 ounces) condensed cream of chicken soup, undiluted
3 tablespoons all-purpose flour
1/4 teaspoon pepper
Dash cayenne pepper
1 pound boneless skinless chicken breasts, cut into cubes
1 celery rib, chopped
1/2 cup chopped green pepper
1/4 cup chopped onion
1 package (10 ounces) frozen peas, thawed
2 tablespoons diced pimientos, drained
Hot cooked rice

In a slow cooker, combine soup, flour, pepper and cayenne until smooth. Stir in chicken, celery, green pepper and onion. Cover and cook on low for 7-8 hours or until meat juices run clear. Stir in peas and pimientos. Cook 30 minutes longer or until heated through. Serve over rice. **Yield:** 6 servings.

Chicken in Mushroom Sauce

Cook Time: 4 to 5 Hours

Kathy Gallagher, La Crosse, Wisconsin

Bacon and sour cream add richness to a simple sauce that really dresses up everyday chicken.

4 boneless skinless chicken breast halves
1 can (10-3/4 ounces) condensed cream of mushroom soup, undiluted

1 cup (8 ounces) sour cream
4 bacon strips, cooked and crumbled

Place chicken in a slow cooker. Combine soup and sour cream; pour over chicken. Cover and cook on low for 4-5 hours or until chicken is tender. Sprinkle with bacon. **Yield:** 4 servings.

Herbed Chicken and Shrimp

(Pictured below)

Cook Time: 4-1/2 to 5-1/2 Hours

Diana Knight, Reno, Nevada

Tender chicken and shrimp make a flavorful combination that's easy to prepare, yet elegant enough to serve at a dinner party. While I clean the house, it practically cooks itself. I serve it over hot cooked rice with crusty bread and a green salad.

1 teaspoon salt
1 teaspoon pepper
1 broiler/fryer chicken (3 to 4 pounds), cut up and skin removed
1/4 cup butter *or* margarine
1 large onion, chopped
1 can (8 ounces) tomato sauce
1/2 cup white wine *or* chicken broth
1 garlic clove, minced
1 teaspoon dried basil
1 pound uncooked medium shrimp, peeled and deveined

Combine salt and pepper; rub over the chicken pieces. In a skillet, brown chicken on all sides in butter. Transfer to an ungreased 5-qt. slow cooker. In a bowl, combine the onion, tomato sauce, wine or

Ham 'n' Swiss Chicken

broth, garlic and basil; pour over chicken. Cover and cook on low for 4-5 hours or until chicken juices run clear. Stir in shrimp. Cover and cook on high for 20-30 minutes or until shrimp turn pink. **Yield:** 4 servings.

Ham 'n' Swiss Chicken

(Pictured above)

Cook Time: 4 to 5 Hours

Dorothy Witmer, Ephrata, Pennsylvania

This saucy casserole allows you to enjoy all the rich flavor of traditional chicken cordon bleu with less effort. It's a snap to layer the ingredients and let them cook all afternoon. Just toss a salad to make this meal complete.

2 eggs
2 cups milk, *divided*
1/2 cup butter *or* margarine, melted
1/2 cup chopped celery
1 teaspoon finely chopped onion
8 slices bread, cubed
12 thin slices deli ham, rolled up
2 cups (8 ounces) shredded Swiss cheese
2-1/2 cups cubed cooked chicken
1 can (10-3/4 ounces) condensed cream of chicken soup, undiluted

In a large bowl, beat the eggs and 1-1/2 cups milk. Add butter, celery and onion. Stir in bread cubes. Place half of the mixture in a greased slow cooker; top with half of the rolled-up ham, cheese and chicken. Combine soup and remaining milk; pour half over the chicken. Repeat layers once.

Cover and cook on low for 4-5 hours or until a thermometer inserted into bread mixture reads 160°. **Yield:** 6 servings.

Herbed Chicken and Shrimp

Herbed Chicken and Veggies

(Pictured below and on page 60)

Cook Time: 8 to 9 Hours

Dorothy Pritchett, Wills Point, Texas

This subtly seasoned chicken and vegetable combination is a snap to prepare on a hectic working day. A dessert is all that's needed to complete this satisfying supper.

- 1 broiler/fryer chicken (3 to 4 pounds), cut up and skin removed
- 2 medium tomatoes, chopped
- 1 medium onion, chopped
- 2 garlic cloves, minced
- 1/2 cup chicken broth
- 2 tablespoons white wine *or* additional chicken broth
- 1 bay leaf
- 1-1/2 teaspoons salt
- 1 teaspoon dried thyme
- 1/4 teaspoon pepper
- 2 cups broccoli florets
- Hot cooked rice

Place chicken in a slow cooker. Top with tomatoes, onion and garlic. Combine broth, wine or additional broth, bay leaf, salt, thyme and pepper; pour over chicken. Cover and cook on low for 7-8 hours. Add broccoli; cook 45-60 minutes longer or until the chicken juices run clear and the broccoli is tender. Discard bay leaf. Thicken pan juices if desired. Serve over rice. **Yield:** 4-6 servings.

Mandarin Chicken

Cook Time: 7-1/2 to 8-1/2 Hours

Aney Chatterton, Soda Springs, Idaho

Oranges and olives are elegantly paired in this different but delicious dish. The chicken is marinated, then cooked slowly in a flavorful sauce, so it stays moist.

- 1 broiler/fryer chicken (3 to 3-1/2 pounds), cut up and skin removed
- 2 cups water
- 1 cup ketchup
- 1/4 cup packed brown sugar
- 1/4 cup soy sauce
- 1/4 cup orange juice concentrate
- 2 teaspoons ground mustard
- 2 teaspoons salt
- 1 teaspoon pepper
- 1 teaspoon ground ginger
- 1 teaspoon garlic salt
- 3 tablespoons cornstarch
- 1/2 cup cold water
- 1 can (11 ounces) mandarin oranges, drained
- 1/2 cup whole pitted ripe olives
- 2 tablespoons chopped green pepper
- Hot cooked rice

Herbed Chicken and Veggies

Slow-Cooked Oriental Chicken

Place chicken in a large resealable plastic bag or glass dish. In a bowl, combine water, ketchup, brown sugar, soy sauce, orange juice concentrate, mustard, salt, pepper, ginger and garlic salt. Pour half over the chicken. Cover chicken and remaining marinade; refrigerate for 8 hours or overnight. Drain chicken, discarding marinade.

Place chicken in a slow cooker; add reserved marinade. Cover and cook on low for 7-8 hours. Combine cornstarch and cold water until smooth; stir into the chicken mixture. Add oranges, olives and green pepper. Cover and cook on high for 30-45 minutes or until thickened. Serve over rice. **Yield:** 4-6 servings.

Slow-Cooked Oriental Chicken

(Pictured above)

Cook Time: 5 to 6 Hours

Ruth Seitz, Columbus Junction, Iowa

Extremely tender chicken is smothered in a flavorful dark gravy in this easy and special entree. It's so nice to find another tantalizing way to serve chicken. Sprinkled with almonds, this is a dish I proudly serve to family or guests.

      1 broiler/fryer chicken (3-1/2 to 4 pounds),
        cut up
      2 tablespoons vegetable oil
  1/3 cup soy sauce
      2 tablespoons brown sugar
      2 tablespoons water
      1 garlic clove, minced
      1 teaspoon ground ginger
  1/4 cup slivered almonds

In a large skillet over medium heat, brown the chicken in oil on both sides. Transfer to a slow cooker. Combine the soy sauce, brown sugar, water, garlic and ginger; pour over chicken. Cover and cook on high for 1 hour. Reduce heat to low; cook 4-5 hours longer or until the meat juices run clear. Remove

chicken to a serving platter; sprinkle with almonds. Spoon juices over chicken or thicken if desired. **Yield:** 4-6 servings.

Slow-Cooked Chicken and Stuffing

(Pictured below)

Cook Time: 4-1/2 to 5 Hours

Angie Marquart, New Washington, Ohio

Prepared in a slow cooker, this tasty no-fuss main dish has a flavorful blend of seasonings and the irresistible duo of tender chicken and moist dressing. It's nice enough for the holidays and easy enough to fix year-round.

  2-1/2 cups chicken broth
      1 cup butter *or* margarine
  1/2 cup chopped onion
  1/2 cup chopped celery
      1 can (4 ounces) mushroom stems and pieces,
        drained
  1/4 cup dried parsley flakes
  1-1/2 teaspoons rubbed sage
      1 teaspoon poultry seasoning
      1 teaspoon salt
  1/2 teaspoon pepper
    12 cups day-old bread cubes (1/2-inch pieces)
      2 eggs
      1 can (10-3/4 ounces) condensed cream of
        chicken soup, undiluted
      5 to 6 cups cubed cooked chicken

In a saucepan, combine the first 10 ingredients. Simmer for 10 minutes; remove from the heat. Place bread cubes in a large bowl. Combine eggs and soup; stir into broth mixture until smooth. Pour over bread and toss well. In a 5-qt. slow cooker, layer half of the stuffing and chicken; repeat layers. Cover and cook on low for 4-1/2 to 5 hours or until a meat thermometer inserted into the stuffing reads 160°. **Yield:** 14-16 servings.

Slow-Cooked Chicken
and Stuffing

Creamy Italian Chicken

Cook Time: 4 Hours

Maura McGee, Tallahassee, Florida

This tender chicken in a creamy sauce gets fast flavor from a salad dressing mix. Served over rice or pasta, it's rich, delicious and special enough for company.

> 4 boneless skinless chicken breast halves
> 1 envelope Italian salad dressing mix
> 1/4 cup water
> 1 package (8 ounces) cream cheese, softened
> 1 can (10-3/4 ounces) condensed cream of chicken soup, undiluted
> 1 can (4 ounces) mushroom stems and pieces, drained

Hot cooked rice *or* noodles

Place the chicken in a slow cooker. Combine salad dressing mix and water; pour over chicken. Cover and cook on low for 3 hours. In a small mixing bowl, beat cream cheese and soup until blended. Stir in mushrooms. Pour over chicken. Cook 1 hour longer or until chicken juices run clear. Serve over rice or noodles. **Yield:** 4 servings.

Tangy Tender Chicken

Cook Time: 8-1/2 to 9-1/2 Hours

Milton Schutz, Pandora, Ohio

Brown sugar, garlic and ginger provide the traditional sweet-sour flavor in this chicken medley. After working outside all day, it's comforting to come home to the heavenly aroma of this simmering supper.

> 1 pound baby carrots
> 1 medium green pepper, cut into 1/2-inch strips
> 1 medium onion, cut into wedges
> 6 boneless skinless chicken breast halves
> 1 can (20 ounces) pineapple chunks
> 1/3 cup packed brown sugar
> 1 tablespoon soy sauce
> 2 teaspoons chicken bouillon granules
> 1/2 teaspoon salt
> 1/2 teaspoon ground ginger
> 1/4 teaspoon garlic powder
> 3 tablespoons cornstarch
> 1/4 cup cold water

Hot cooked rice

Turkey with Mushroom Sauce

Turkey with Mushroom Sauce

(Pictured above)

Cook Time: 7 to 8 Hours

Myra Innes, Auburn, Kansas

When we were first married, I didn't have an oven, so I made this tender turkey in the slow cooker. Now I rely on this recipe because it frees up the oven to make other dishes.

> 1 boneless turkey breast (3 pounds), halved
> 2 tablespoons butter *or* margarine, melted
> 2 tablespoons dried parsley flakes
> 1/2 teaspoon dried tarragon
> 1/2 teaspoon salt
> 1/8 teaspoon pepper
> 1 jar (4-1/2 ounces) sliced mushrooms, drained *or* 1 cup sliced fresh mushrooms
> 1/2 cup white wine *or* chicken broth
> 2 tablespoons cornstarch
> 1/4 cup cold water

Place the turkey, skin side up, in a slow cooker. Brush with butter. Sprinkle with parsley, tarragon, salt and pepper. Top with mushrooms. Pour wine or broth over all. Cover and cook on low for 7-8 hours. Remove turkey and keep warm. Skim fat from cooking juices.

In a saucepan, combine the cornstarch and water until smooth. Gradually add the cooking juices. Bring to a boil; cook and stir for 2 minutes or until thickened. Serve with the turkey. **Yield:** 8 servings.

You've Got Good Taste

Always taste the finished dish before serving to adjust seasonings to your preference, since long cooking times can dilute the strength of herbs and spices. Consider adding a dash of salt, pepper, lemon juice or minced fresh herbs.

In a slow cooker, layer carrots, green pepper and onion. Top with the chicken. Drain pineapple, reserving juice. Place pineapple over chicken. Add brown sugar, soy sauce, bouillon, salt, ginger and garlic powder to pineapple juice; pour over pineapple. Cover and cook on low for 8-9 hours.

Combine cornstarch and water until smooth; gradually stir into cooking juices. Cook 30 minutes longer or until sauce is thickened, stirring once. Serve over rice. **Yield:** 4-6 servings.

Saucy Apricot Chicken

(Pictured below)

Cook Time: 4 to 5 Hours

Dee Gray, Kokomo, Indiana

Just four ingredients are all you'll need for a scrumptious chicken entree. The tangy glaze is just as wonderful with ham or turkey. Leftovers of this dish reheat nicely in the microwave.

>   **6 boneless skinless chicken breast halves**
>   **(about 1-1/2 pounds)**
>   **2 jars (12 ounces *each*) apricot preserves**
>   **1 envelope onion soup mix**
> **Hot cooked rice**

Place chicken in a slow cooker. Combine the preserves and soup mix; spoon over chicken. Cover and cook on low for 4-5 hours or until tender. Serve over rice. **Yield:** 6 servings.

Slow-Cooked Lemon Chicken

Slow-Cooked Lemon Chicken

(Pictured above)

Cook Time: 3-1/2 to 4-1/2 Hours

Walter Powell, Wilmington, Delaware

Garlic, oregano and lemon juice give spark to this memorable main dish. It's easy to prepare—just brown the chicken in a skillet, then let the slow cooker do the work. I'm proud to serve this dish to company.

>   **6 bone-in chicken breast halves (about 3**
>   **pounds), skin removed**
>   **1 teaspoon dried oregano**
>   **1/2 teaspoon seasoned salt**
>   **1/4 teaspoon pepper**
>   **2 tablespoons butter *or* margarine**
>   **1/4 cup water**
>   **3 tablespoons lemon juice**
>   **2 garlic cloves, minced**
>   **1 teaspoon chicken bouillon granules**
>   **2 teaspoons minced fresh parsley**
> **Hot cooked rice**

Pat the chicken dry with paper towels. Combine the oregano, seasoned salt and pepper; rub over the chicken. In a skillet over medium heat, brown the chicken in butter; transfer to a 5-qt. slow cooker. Add the water, lemon juice, garlic and bouillon to the skillet; bring to a boil, stirring to loosen browned bits. Pour over chicken. Cover and cook on low for 3-4 hours.

Baste the chicken. Add parsley. Cover and cook 15-30 minutes longer or until meat juices run clear. If desired, thicken cooking juices and serve over chicken and rice. **Yield:** 6 servings.

Saucy Apricot Chicken

Sweet and Tangy Chicken

Cook Time: 8 to 9 Hours

Mary Zawlocki, Gig Harbor, Washington

Spicy barbecue sauce blends with sweet pineapple in this quick-to-fix chicken dish. It's tasty enough for a company dinner…just add a salad and rolls.

- 8 boneless skinless chicken breast halves
- 2 bottles (18 ounces *each*) barbecue sauce
- 1 can (20 ounces) pineapple chunks, undrained
- 1 medium green pepper, chopped
- 1 medium onion, chopped
- 2 garlic cloves, minced
- Hot cooked rice

Place four chicken breasts in a 5-qt. slow cooker. Combine barbecue sauce, pineapple, green pepper, onion and garlic; pour half over the chicken. Top with remaining chicken and sauce. Cover and cook on low for 8-9 hours or until chicken is tender. Thicken sauce if desired. Serve the chicken and sauce over rice. **Yield:** 8 servings.

Stuffed Chicken Rolls

(Pictured below)

Cook Time: 4 to 5 Hours

Jean Sherwood, Kenneth City, Florida

The wonderful aroma of this moist delicious chicken cooking sparks our appetites. The ham and cheese rolled inside is a tasty surprise. When I prepared this impressive main dish for a church luncheon, I received lots of compliments. The rolls are especially nice served over rice or pasta.

- 6 boneless skinless chicken breast halves
- 6 slices fully cooked ham
- 6 slices Swiss cheese
- 1/4 cup all-purpose flour
- 1/4 cup grated Parmesan cheese
- 1/2 teaspoon rubbed sage
- 1/4 teaspoon paprika
- 1/4 teaspoon pepper
- 1/4 cup vegetable oil
- 1 can (10-3/4 ounces) condensed cream of chicken soup, undiluted
- 1/2 cup chicken broth
- Chopped fresh parsley, optional

Flatten chicken to 1/8-in. thickness. Place ham and cheese on each breast. Roll up and tuck in ends; secure with a toothpick. Combine the flour, Parmesan cheese, sage, paprika and pepper; coat chicken on all sides. Cover and refrigerate for 1 hour.

In a large skillet, brown chicken in oil over medium-high heat. Transfer to a 5-qt. slow cooker. Combine soup and broth; pour over chicken. Cover and cook on low for 4-5 hours. Remove toothpicks. Garnish with parsley if desired. **Yield:** 6 servings.

Turkey with Cranberry Sauce

Cook Time: 4 to 6 Hours

Marie Ramsden, Fairgrove, Michigan

This is a very tasty and easy way to cook turkey in the slow cooker. The sweet cranberry sauce complements the turkey nicely.

- 2 boneless skinless turkey breast halves (about 4 pounds *each*)
- 1 can (14 ounces) jellied cranberry sauce
- 1/2 cup plus 2 tablespoons water, *divided*
- 1 envelope onion soup mix
- 2 tablespoons cornstarch

Cut each turkey breast in half; place in a 5-qt. slow cooker. In a bowl, combine the cranberry sauce, 1/2 cup water and soup mix; mix well. Pour over the turkey. Cover and cook on low for 4-6 hours or until the turkey is no longer pink and a meat thermometer reads 170°. Remove turkey and keep warm. Trans-

Stuffed Chicken Rolls

Creamy Chicken Fettuccine

and pimientos if desired. Cover and cook until the cheese is melted.

Meanwhile, cook fettuccine according to package directions; drain. Serve with the chicken and breadsticks if desired. **Yield:** 6 servings.

Rosemary Cashew Chicken

(Pictured below)

Cook Time: 4 to 5 Hours

Ruth Andrewson, Peck, Idaho

This elegant entree with fresh herb flavor is mouth-watering. Cashews add richness and crunch.

> 1 broiler/fryer chicken (3 to 4 pounds), cut up and skin removed
> 1 medium onion, thinly sliced
> 1/3 cup orange juice concentrate
> 1 teaspoon dried rosemary, crushed
> 1 teaspoon salt
> 1/4 teaspoon cayenne pepper
> 2 tablespoons all-purpose flour
> 3 tablespoons water
> 1/4 to 1/2 cup chopped cashews

Hot cooked pasta

Place chicken in a slow cooker. Combine onion, orange juice concentrate, rosemary, salt and cayenne; pour over chicken. Cover and cook on low for 4-5 hours or until chicken juices run clear. Remove the chicken and keep warm.

In a saucepan, combine flour and water until smooth. Stir in cooking juices. Bring to a boil; cook and stir for 2 minutes or until thickened. Stir in cashews. Pour over chicken. Serve with pasta. **Yield:** 4-6 servings.

fer the cranberry mixture to a small saucepan.

In a bowl, combine the cornstarch and remaining water until smooth. Bring cranberry mixture to a boil; stir in cornstarch mixture. Cook and stir for 2 minutes or until thickened. Slice turkey; serve with cranberry sauce. **Yield:** 20-25 servings.

Creamy Chicken Fettuccine

(Pictured above)

Cook Time: 3 to 4 Hours

Melissa Cowser, Greenville, Texas

Convenient canned soup and process American cheese hurry along the assembly of this creamy sauce loaded with delicious chunks of chicken.

> 1-1/2 pounds boneless skinless chicken breasts, cut into cubes
> 1/2 teaspoon garlic powder
> 1/2 teaspoon onion powder
> 1/8 teaspoon pepper
> 1 can (10-3/4 ounces) condensed cream of chicken soup, undiluted
> 1 can (10-3/4 ounces) condensed cream of celery soup, undiluted
> 4 ounces process American cheese, cubed
> 1 can (2-1/4 ounces) sliced ripe olives, drained
> 1 jar (2 ounces) diced pimientos, drained, optional
> 1 package (16 ounces) spinach fettuccine *or* spaghetti

Thin breadsticks, optional

Place the chicken in a slow cooker; sprinkle with garlic powder, onion powder and pepper. Top with soups. Cover and cook on high for 3-4 hours or until chicken juices run clear. Stir in the cheese, olives

Rosemary Cashew Chicken

Tender Barbecued Chicken

Cook Time: 8 to10 Hours

Jacqueline Blanton, Gaffney, South Carolina

I'm a teacher and work most of the day, so slow-cooked meals are a great help. One of my family's favorites is this moist slow-simmered chicken. For an appealing look, choose a darker brown barbecue sauce.

    1 broiler/fryer chicken (3 to 4 pounds), cut up
    1 medium onion, thinly sliced
    1 medium lemon, thinly sliced
    1 bottle (18 ounces) barbecue sauce*
    3/4 cup regular cola

Place chicken in a slow cooker. Top with onion and lemon slices. Combine barbecue sauce and cola; pour over all. Cover and cook on low for 8-10 hours or until chicken juices run clear. **Yield:** 4-6 servings.

*Editor's Note: This recipe was tested with K.C. Masterpiece brand barbecue sauce.

Chicken Cacciatore

(Pictured below)

Cook Time: 6 to 8 Hours

Aggie Arnold-Norman, Liberty, Pennsylvania

My husband and I milk 125 cows. There are days when there's just no time left for cooking! It's really nice to be able to come in from the barn at night and smell this meal simmering—dinner is a simple matter of dishing it up. I've used this recipe for many years, and everyone who tries it likes it. It's very easy to make, but it's also special enough to serve to company.

    2 medium onions, thinly sliced
    1 broiler/fryer chicken (2-1/2 to 3 pounds), cut up and skin removed

Chicken Cacciatore

    2 garlic cloves, minced
    1 to 2 teaspoons dried oregano
    1 teaspoon salt
    1/2 teaspoon dried basil
    1/4 teaspoon pepper
    1 bay leaf
    1 can (14-1/2 ounces) diced tomatoes
    1 can (8 ounces) tomato sauce
    1 can (4 ounces) mushroom stems and pieces, drained *or* 1 cup sliced fresh mushrooms
    1/4 cup dry white wine *or* water
Hot cooked pasta

Place sliced onions in a 5-qt. slow cooker. Add the chicken, seasonings, tomatoes, sauce, mushrooms and wine or water. Cover; cook on low for 6-8 hours or until chicken juices run clear. Discard bay leaf. Serve chicken with sauce over pasta. **Yield:** 6 servings.

Creamy Chicken and Beef

Cook Time: 8 to 9 Hours

Jane Thocher, Hart, Michigan

Bacon and canned cream of mushroom soup dress up this tender chicken entree. I relied on this dish often when our children lived at home. Since it cooked while I was at work, the only thing left to do was prepare noodles and fix a salad.

    6 bacon strips
    1 package (2-1/2 ounces) thinly sliced dried beef
    6 boneless skinless chicken breast halves
    1/4 cup all-purpose flour
    1 can (10-3/4 ounces) condensed cream of mushroom soup, undiluted
    1/4 cup sour cream
Hot cooked noodles

In a skillet, partially cook bacon over medium heat. Drain on paper towels. Place beef in a greased slow cooker. Fold chicken pieces in half and wrap a bacon strip around each; place over the beef. Combine the flour, soup and sour cream until blended; spread over chicken. Cover and cook on low for 8-9 hours or until chicken juices run clear. Serve over noodles. **Yield:** 6 servings.

King-Size Drumsticks

Cook Time: 8 to 10 Hours

Let your slow cooker do the work for you when these savory turkey legs make an appearance on your dinner table. In a recipe generated by our Test Kitchen, canned enchilada sauce, green chilies and cumin give this main dish a zesty royal treatment.

    1 can (10 ounces) enchilada sauce
    1 can (4 ounces) chopped green chilies, drained
    1 teaspoon dried oregano
    1/2 teaspoon garlic salt
    1/2 teaspoon ground cumin
    6 turkey drumsticks
    3 tablespoons cornstarch
    3 tablespoons cold water

In a bowl, combine the enchilada sauce, chilies, oregano, garlic salt and cumin. Place the drumsticks in a 5-qt. slow cooker; top with sauce. Cover and cook on low for 8-10 hours or until a meat thermometer reads 180°.

Remove turkey and keep warm. Strain sauce into a saucepan. Combine the cornstarch and water until smooth; stir into the pan. Bring to a boil; cook and stir for 2 minutes or until thickened. Serve with turkey. **Yield:** 6 servings.

Sunday Chicken Supper

(Pictured above and on front cover)

Cook Time: 6 to 8 Hours

Ruthann Martin, Louisville, Ohio

This slow-cooked sensation is loaded with chicken, vegetables and seasonings. It's a dish that satisfies the biggest appetites.

> 4 medium carrots, cut into 2-inch pieces
> 1 medium onion, chopped
> 1 celery rib, cut into 2-inch pieces
> 2 cups cut fresh green beans (2-inch pieces)
> 5 small red potatoes, quartered
> 2 to 4 tablespoons vegetable oil
> 1 broiler/fryer chicken (3 to 3-1/2 pounds), cut up
> 4 bacon strips, cooked and crumbled
> 1-1/2 cups hot water
> 2 teaspoons chicken bouillon granules
> 1 teaspoon salt
> 1/2 teaspoon dried thyme
> 1/2 teaspoon dried basil
> Pinch pepper

In a 5-qt. slow cooker, layer the first five ingredients in order listed. In a large skillet, heat oil; brown the chicken on all sides. Transfer to a slow cooker; top with the bacon.

In a bowl, combine the remaining ingredients; pour over the top. Do not stir. Cover and cook on low for 6-8 hours or until vegetables are tender and chicken juices run clear. Remove chicken and vegetables. If desired, thicken juices for gravy in a saucepan. Return chicken and vegetables to slow cooker. Drizzle with gravy. **Yield:** 4 servings.

Pork & Ham

Sweet 'n' Sour Ribs (p. 83)

Chapter 6

Chalupa

(Pictured below)

Cook Time: 8 Hours

Ginny Becker, Torrington, Wyoming

This is such a refreshing change of pace from traditional chili. It's also fun to serve to guests. Nearly everyone who's sampled it has requested the recipe.

    1 cup dried pinto beans
3-1/2 cups water
    1/4 cup chopped onion
    1 can (4 ounces) chopped green chilies
    1 garlic clove, minced
    1 tablespoon chili powder
1-1/2 teaspoons salt
1-1/2 teaspoons ground cumin
    1/2 teaspoon dried oregano
    1 boneless pork shoulder roast (1-1/2 pounds), trimmed
    1 package (10-1/2 ounces) corn chips
    1/4 cup sliced green onions
Shredded lettuce
Shredded cheddar cheese
Chopped fresh tomatoes
Salsa

Place beans and enough water to cover in a 3-qt. saucepan. Bring to a boil; boil for 2 minutes. Remove from the heat; let stand for 1 hour. Drain beans and discard liquid. In a slow cooker, combine water, onion, chilies, garlic, chili powder, salt, cumin and oregano. Add roast and beans. Cover and cook on high for 2 hours. Reduce heat to low and cook 6 hours longer or until pork is very tender.

Remove roast and shred with a fork. Drain beans, reserving cooking liquid in a saucepan. Combine beans and meat; set aside. Skim and discard fat from cooking liquid; bring to a boil. Boil, uncovered, for 20 minutes or until reduced to 1-1/2 cups. Add meat and bean mixture; heat through. Spoon meat mixture over corn chips; top with green onions, lettuce, cheese, tomatoes and salsa. **Yield:** 6-8 servings.

Orange Pork Roast

Cook Time: 6 to 8 Hours

Nancy Medeiros, Sparks, Nevada

Overcooking can cause pork roasts to be dry and tough. But slow cooking and this recipe's succulent orange sauce guarantee that the meat turns out moist and tender.

    1 pork shoulder roast (3 to 4 pounds), trimmed
    1/2 teaspoon salt
    1/8 teaspoon pepper
    1 can (6 ounces) frozen orange juice concentrate, thawed
    1/4 cup honey
    1/8 teaspoon ground cloves
    1/8 teaspoon ground nutmeg
    3 tablespoons all-purpose flour
    1/4 cup cold water

Sprinkle roast with salt and pepper; place in a slow cooker. Combine orange juice concentrate, honey, cloves and nutmeg; pour over pork. Cover and cook on high for 2 hours. Reduce heat to low and cook 6 hours longer. Remove meat to a serving platter; cover and keep warm.

Skim and discard fat from cooking liquid; pour into a saucepan. Combine flour and cold water until smooth; stir into cooking liquid. Bring to a boil; stir for 2 minutes. Serve with roast. **Yield:** 8 servings.

Chicken Fried Chops

Cook Time: 6 to 8 Hours

Connie Slocum, Brunswick, Georgia

It takes only a few minutes to brown the meat before assembling this savory meal. The pork chops simmer all day in a flavorful sauce until they're fork-tender.

    1/2 cup all-purpose flour
    2 teaspoons salt
1-1/2 teaspoons ground mustard
    1/2 teaspoon garlic powder
    6 pork loin chops (3/4 inch thick), trimmed
    2 tablespoons vegetable oil
    1 can (10-3/4 ounces) condensed cream of chicken soup, undiluted
    1/3 cup water

In a shallow bowl, combine flour, salt, mustard and garlic powder; dredge pork chops. In a skillet, brown the chops on both sides in oil. Place in a slow cooker. Combine soup and water; pour over chops. Cover and cook on low for 6-8 hours or until meat is tender. If desired, thicken pan juices and serve with the pork chops. **Yield:** 6 servings.

Chalupa

Sunday Pot Roast

bine the flour and water until smooth; stir into broth. Bring to a boil; boil and whisk for 2 minutes. Add the browning sauce if desired. Serve with the roast. **Yield:** 12-14 servings.

Ham with Cherry Sauce

(Pictured below)

Cook Time: 4 to 5 Hours

Carol Lee Jones, Taylors, South Carolina

I'm always happy to fix this delicious ham topped with a thick cherry sauce. It's such a favorite that I've served it at Easter dinners, church breakfasts and a friend's wedding brunch.

    1 boneless fully cooked ham (3 to 4 pounds)
  1/2 cup apple jelly
    2 teaspoons prepared mustard
  2/3 cup ginger ale, *divided*
    1 can (21 ounces) cherry pie filling
    2 tablespoons cornstarch

Score surface of ham, making diamond shapes 1/2 in. deep. In a small bowl, combine jelly, mustard and 1 tablespoon ginger ale; rub over scored surface of ham. Cut ham in half; place in a 5-qt. slow cooker. Cover and cook on low for 4-5 hours or until a meat thermometer reads 140° and ham is heated through. Baste with cooking juices toward end of cooking.

For sauce, place pie filling in a saucepan. Combine cornstarch and remaining ginger ale; stir into pie filling until blended. Bring to a boil; cook and stir for 2 minutes or until thickened. Serve over ham. **Yield:** 12-16 servings.

Sunday Pot Roast

(Pictured above)

Cook Time: 8 Hours

Brandy Schaefer, Glen Carbon, Illinois

This recipe proves you don't have to slave over a hot stove to prepare a delicious down-home dinner like Grandma used to make. The roast turns out moist and tasty every time.

      1 teaspoon dried oregano
    1/2 teaspoon onion salt
    1/2 teaspoon pepper
    1/2 teaspoon caraway seed
    1/4 teaspoon garlic salt
      1 boneless pork loin roast (3-1/2 to 4 pounds),
        trimmed
      6 medium carrots, peeled and cut into
        1-1/2-inch pieces
      3 large potatoes, peeled and quartered
      3 small onions, quartered
  1-1/2 cups beef broth
    1/3 cup all-purpose flour
    1/3 cup cold water
    1/4 teaspoon browning sauce, optional

Combine the seasonings; rub over roast. Wrap in plastic wrap and refrigerate overnight. Place carrots, potatoes and onions in a slow cooker; add broth. Unwrap roast and place in the slow cooker. Cover and cook on high for 2 hours. Reduce heat to low and cook 6 hours longer.

Transfer the roast and vegetables to a serving platter; keep warm. Pour broth into a saucepan. Com-

Ham with Cherry Sauce

Mushroom Pork Tenderloin

Cook Time: 4 to 5 Hours

Donna Hughes, Rochester, New Hampshire

This moist pork tenderloin in a savory gravy is the best you'll ever taste. Prepared with canned soups, it couldn't be easier to assemble. It's a comforting main dish any time of year.

2 pork tenderloins (1 pound *each***)**
1 can (10-3/4 ounces) condensed cream of mushroom soup, undiluted
1 can (10-3/4 ounces) condensed golden mushroom soup, undiluted
1 can (10-1/2 ounces) condensed French onion soup, undiluted
Hot mashed potatoes, optional

Place pork in a slow cooker. In a bowl, combine the soups; stir until smooth. Pour over pork. Cover and cook on low for 4-5 hours or until the meat is tender. Serve with mashed potatoes if desired. **Yield:** 6 servings.

Tender 'n' Tangy Ribs

(Pictured below)

Cook Time: 4 to 6 Hours

Denise Hathaway Valasek, Perrysburg, Ohio

These ribs are so simple to prepare. Just brown them, then combine with the sauce ingredients in your slow cooker. Serve them at noon…or let them cook all day for falling-off-the-bone tenderness.

Tender 'n' Tangy Ribs

3/4 to 1 cup vinegar
1/2 cup ketchup
2 tablespoons sugar
2 tablespoons Worcestershire sauce
1 garlic clove, minced
1 teaspoon ground mustard
1 teaspoon paprika
1/2 to 1 teaspoon salt
1/8 teaspoon pepper
2 pounds pork spareribs
1 tablespoon vegetable oil

Combine the first nine ingredients in a slow cooker. Cut ribs into serving-size pieces; brown in a skillet in oil. Transfer to slow cooker. Cover and cook on low for 4-6 hours or until tender. **Yield:** 2-3 servings.

Pork and Cabbage Dinner

Cook Time: 8 Hours

Trina Hinkel, Minneapolis, Minnesota

I put on this pork roast in the morning to avoid that evening dinner rush. All I do is fix potatoes, and our family can sit down to a satisfying supper.

1 pound carrots
1-1/2 cups water
1 envelope onion soup mix
2 garlic cloves, minced
1/2 teaspoon celery seed
1 boneless pork shoulder roast (4 to 6 pounds)
1/2 teaspoon salt
1/4 teaspoon pepper
1-1/2 pounds cabbage, cut into 2-inch pieces

Cut carrots in half lengthwise and then into 2-in. pieces. Place in a 5-qt. slow cooker. Add water, soup mix, garlic and celery seed. Cut roast in half; place over carrot mixture. Sprinkle with salt and pepper. Cover and cook on high for 2 hours.

Reduce heat to low; cook for 4 hours. Add cabbage; cook 2 hours longer or until the cabbage is tender and a meat thermometer reads 160°. Remove meat and vegetables to a serving plate; keep warm. If desired, thicken pan drippings for gravy and serve with the roast. **Yield:** 8-10 servings.

Creamy Ham and Potatoes

Cook Time: 8 to 9 Hours

Peggy Key, Grant, Alabama

Serve this stick-to-your-ribs dish with a green salad and dessert for a complete meal. The creamy mixture of hearty ham and tender potatoes is brimming with homemade flavor.

4 medium red potatoes, thinly sliced
2 medium onions, finely chopped
1-1/2 cups cubed fully cooked ham
2 tablespoons butter *or* **margarine**
2 tablespoons all-purpose flour
1 teaspoon ground mustard
1/2 teaspoon salt
1/2 teaspoon pepper

1 can (10-3/4 ounces) condensed cream of
    celery soup, undiluted
1-1/3 cups water
1 cup (4 ounces) shredded cheddar cheese,
    optional

In a slow cooker, layer potatoes, onions and ham. In
a saucepan, melt butter. Stir in flour, mustard, salt
and pepper until smooth. Combine soup and water;
gradually stir into flour mixture. Bring to a boil; cook
and stir for 2 minutes or until thickened and bubbly. Pour over ham.

Cover and cook on low for 8-9 hours or until potatoes are tender. If desired, sprinkle with cheese before serving. **Yield:** 4 servings.

Pork Carnitas

Cook Time: 9 to 11 Hours

Tracy Byers, Corvallis, Oregon

*I use this recipe often when entertaining. I set out all the top-
pings, and folks have fun assembling their own carnitas. Because
I can prepare everything in advance, I get to spend more time
with my guests.*

1 boneless pork shoulder *or* loin roast (2 to 3
    pounds), trimmed and cut into 3-inch cubes
1/2 cup lime juice
1 teaspoon salt
1/2 teaspoon pepper
1/2 teaspoon crushed red pepper flakes
12 flour tortillas (7 inches), warmed
2 cups (8 ounces) shredded cheddar *or*
    Monterey Jack cheese
2 medium avocados, peeled and diced
2 medium tomatoes, diced
1 medium onion, diced
Shredded lettuce
Minced fresh cilantro, optional
Salsa

In a slow cooker, combine the pork, lime juice, salt,
pepper and pepper flakes. Cover and cook on high
for 1 hour; stir. Reduce heat to low and cook 8-10
hours longer or until the meat is very tender.

Shred the pork with a fork (it may look somewhat
pink). Spoon about 1/3 cup of the filling down the
center of each tortilla; top with cheese, avocados,
tomatoes, onion, lettuce and cilantro if desired. Fold
in bottom and sides of tortilla. Serve with salsa.
Yield: 12 servings.

Avoiding a Sticky Situation

*Slow cooker inserts are fairly easy to clean
with hot soapy water. For even faster cleanup, coat the bottom and sides of the insert
with nonstick cooking spray before putting
in the food.*

Tangy Pork Chops

Tangy Pork Chops

(Pictured above)

Cook Time: 5-1/2 to 6-1/2 Hours

Karol Hines, Kitty Hawk, North Carolina

*Fancy enough for company, these mouth-watering pork chops
also make a great family meal. I usually have all the ingredients on hand.*

4 pork chops (1/2 inch thick)
1/2 teaspoon salt
1/8 teaspoon pepper
2 medium onions, chopped
2 celery ribs, chopped
1 large green pepper, sliced
1 can (14-1/2 ounces) stewed tomatoes
1/2 cup ketchup
2 tablespoons cider vinegar
2 tablespoons brown sugar
2 tablespoons Worcestershire sauce
1 tablespoon lemon juice
1 beef bouillon cube
2 tablespoons cornstarch
2 tablespoons water
Hot cooked rice, optional

Place chops in a slow cooker; sprinkle with salt and
pepper. Add the onions, celery, green pepper and
tomatoes. Combine ketchup, vinegar, sugar, Worcestershire sauce, lemon juice and bouillon; pour over
vegetables. Cover and cook on low for 5-6 hours.

Mix cornstarch and water until smooth; stir into
liquid in slow cooker. Cover and cook on high for
30 minutes or until thickened. Serve over rice if desired. **Yield:** 4 servings.

Sausage Sauerkraut Supper

(Pictured at right)

Cook Time: 8 to 9 Hours

Joalyce Graham, St. Petersburg, Florida

With big tender chunks of sausage, potatoes and carrots, this meal-in-one has old-world flavor that will satisfy the heartiest of appetites. A co-worker often made a big pot of this for our office staff, and it always disappeared in a hurry.

4 cups carrot chunks (2-inch pieces)
4 cups red potato chunks
2 cans (14 ounces *each*) sauerkraut, rinsed and drained
2-1/2 pounds fresh Polish sausage, cut into 3-inch pieces
1 medium onion, thinly sliced
3 garlic cloves, minced
1-1/2 cups dry white wine *or* chicken broth
1 teaspoon pepper
1/2 teaspoon caraway seed

In a 5-qt. slow cooker, layer carrots, potatoes and sauerkraut. In a skillet, brown the sausage; transfer to the slow cooker (slow cooker will be full). Reserve 1 tablespoon drippings in skillet; saute onion and garlic until tender. Gradually add wine or broth. Bring to a boil; stir to loosen browned bits. Stir in pepper and caraway. Pour over sausage.

Cover and cook on low for 8-9 hours or until the vegetables are tender and the sausage is no longer pink. **Yield:** 10-12 servings.

Sausage Sauerkraut Supper

Sesame Pork Roast

Cook Time: 9 to 10 Hours

Sue Brown, San Miguel, California

I marinate a boneless cut of pork in a tangy sauce overnight before cooking it slowly the next day. The result is a tasty roast that's fall-apart tender.

1 boneless pork shoulder roast (4 pounds), trimmed
2 cups water
1/2 cup soy sauce
1/4 cup sesame seeds, toasted
1/4 cup molasses
1/4 cup white wine vinegar *or* cider vinegar
4 green onions, sliced
2 teaspoons garlic powder
1/4 teaspoon cayenne pepper
3 tablespoons cornstarch
1/4 cup cold water

Cut roast in half; place in a large resealable plastic bag or glass dish. In a bowl, combine the water, soy sauce, sesame seeds, molasses, vinegar, onions, garlic powder and cayenne. Pour half over the roast. Cover the pork and remaining marinade; refrigerate overnight.

Drain pork, discarding marinade. Place roast in a 5-qt. slow cooker; add the reserved marinade. Cover and cook on high for 1 hour. Reduce tempera-ture to low; cook 8-9 hours longer or until meat is tender. Remove the roast and keep warm. In a saucepan, combine cornstarch and cold water until smooth; stir in cooking juices. Bring to a boil; boil and stir for 2 minutes. **Yield:** 8 servings.

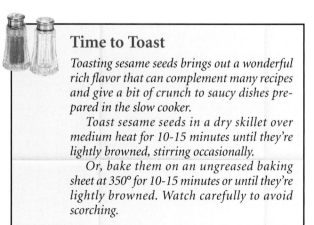

Time to Toast

Toasting sesame seeds brings out a wonderful rich flavor that can complement many recipes and give a bit of crunch to saucy dishes prepared in the slow cooker.

Toast sesame seeds in a dry skillet over medium heat for 10-15 minutes until they're lightly browned, stirring occasionally.

Or, bake them on an ungreased baking sheet at 350° for 10-15 minutes or until they're lightly browned. Watch carefully to avoid scorching.

Hot Dogs 'n' Beans

Cook Time: 7 to 8 Hours

June Formanek, Belle Plaine, Iowa

You'll please kids of all ages with this tasty combination that's good for casual get-togethers. I frequently fix this when the whole family is home.

- 3 cans (two 28 ounces, one 16 ounces) pork and beans
- 1 package (1 pound) hot dogs, halved lengthwise and cut into 1-inch pieces
- 1 large onion, chopped
- 1/2 cup packed brown sugar
- 3 tablespoons prepared mustard
- 4 bacon strips, cooked and crumbled

In a slow cooker, combine all ingredients; mix well. Cover and cook on low for 7-8 hours. **Yield:** 10 servings.

Tender Pork Roast

Cook Time: 8 to 9 Hours

LuVerne Peterson, Minneapolis, Minnesota

This easy melt-in-your-mouth pork roast is wonderful to serve to company because it never fails to please.

- 1 boneless pork roast (about 3 pounds)
- 1 can (8 ounces) tomato sauce
- 3/4 cup soy sauce
- 1/2 cup sugar
- 2 teaspoons ground mustard

Cut roast in half; place in a 5-qt. slow cooker. Combine remaining ingredients; pour over roast. Cover and cook on low for 8-9 hours or until a meat thermometer reads 160°-170°. Remove roast to a serving platter and keep warm. If desired, skim fat from pan juices and thicken for gravy. **Yield:** 8 servings.

Casserole in the Cooker

Cook Time: 4 to 5 Hours

Krista Harrison, Brazil, Indiana

For a complete meal-in-one, you'll savor this slow-cooked ham, broccoli and rice dish that has all the goodness of an oven-baked casserole. It's perfect for a Sunday afternoon dinner.

- 1 package (16 ounces) frozen broccoli cuts, thawed and drained
- 3 cups cubed fully cooked ham
- 1 can (10-3/4 ounces) condensed cream of mushroom soup, undiluted
- 1 jar (8 ounces) process cheese sauce
- 1 cup milk
- 1 cup uncooked instant rice
- 1 celery rib, chopped
- 1 small onion, chopped

In a slow cooker, combine broccoli and ham. Combine the soup, cheese sauce, milk, rice, celery and onion; stir into the broccoli mixture. Cover and cook on low for 4-5 hours or until rice is tender. **Yield:** 4 servings.

Sweet 'n' Sour Ribs

(Pictured below and on page 76)

Cook Time: 8 to 10 Hours

Dorothy Voelz, Champaign, Illinois

If you're looking for a change from typical barbecue ribs, you'll enjoy this recipe my mom always prepared on birthdays and special occasions. The tender ribs have a slight sweet-and-sour taste that my family loves. I usually serve them with garlic mashed potatoes and a salad or coleslaw.

- 3 to 4 pounds boneless country-style pork ribs
- 1 can (20 ounces) pineapple tidbits, undrained
- 2 cans (8 ounces *each*) tomato sauce
- 1/2 cup thinly sliced onion
- 1/2 cup thinly sliced green pepper
- 1/2 cup packed brown sugar
- 1/4 cup cider vinegar
- 1/4 cup tomato paste
- 2 tablespoons Worcestershire sauce
- 1 garlic clove, minced

Salt and pepper to taste

Place the ribs in an ungreased 5-qt. slow cooker. In a bowl, combine the remaining ingredients; pour over the ribs. Cover and cook on low for 8-10 hours or until the meat is tender. Thicken the sauce if desired. **Yield:** 8 servings.

Sweet 'n' Sour Ribs

Pizza in a Pot

Cook Time: 8 to 9 Hours

Anita Doughty, West Des Moines, Iowa

Since most kids will try anything to do with pizza, I rely on this recipe when one of my two teenage sons has a friend stay for dinner. It's frequently a hit.

>   1 pound bulk Italian sausage
>   1 can (28 ounces) crushed tomatoes
>   1 can (15-1/2 ounces) chili beans
>   1 can (15 ounces) black beans, rinsed and
>   drained
>   1 can (2-1/4 ounces) sliced ripe olives, drained
>   1 medium onion, chopped
>   1 small green pepper, chopped
>   2 garlic cloves, minced
> 1/4 cup grated Parmesan cheese
>   1 tablespoon quick-cooking tapioca
>   1 tablespoon dried basil
>   1 bay leaf
>   1 teaspoon salt
> 1/2 teaspoon sugar
> Hot cooked pasta
> Shredded mozzarella cheese, optional

In a skillet over medium heat, cook the sausage until no longer pink; drain. Transfer to a slow cooker. Add the next 13 ingredients; mix well. Cover and cook on low for 8-9 hours or until slightly thickened. Discard bay leaf. Stir before serving over pasta. Sprinkle with mozzarella cheese if desired. **Yield:** 6-8 servings.

Easy and Elegant Ham

Peachy Pork Steaks

Cook Time: 5 Hours

Sandra McKenzie, Braham, Minnesota

My mother has been preparing this delicious pork dish for many years. She always found it a surefire way to get even picky children to eat meat. It seems that no one can refuse these succulent steaks!

>   4 pork steaks (1/2 inch thick), trimmed
>   2 tablespoons vegetable oil
> 3/4 teaspoon dried basil
> 1/4 teaspoon salt
> Dash pepper
>   1 can (15-1/4 ounces) peach slices in heavy
>   syrup, undrained
>   2 tablespoons vinegar
>   1 tablespoon beef bouillon granules
>   2 tablespoons cornstarch
> 1/4 cup cold water
> Hot cooked rice

In a skillet, brown the steaks in oil; sprinkle with basil, salt and pepper. Drain the peaches, reserving juice. Place the peaches in a slow cooker; top with steaks. Combine the juice, vinegar and bouillon; pour over steaks. Cover and cook on high for 1 hour. Reduce heat to low and cook 4 hours longer or until meat is tender. Remove steaks and peaches to a serving platter; keep warm.

Skim and discard fat from cooking liquid; pour into a saucepan. Combine cornstarch and cold water until smooth; stir into cooking liquid. Bring to a boil; boil and stir for 2 minutes. Serve steaks, peaches and sauce over rice. **Yield:** 4 servings.

Easy and Elegant Ham

(Pictured at left)

Cook Time: 6 to 7 Hours

Denise DiPace, Medford, New Jersey

I fix this moist tender ham to serve my large family. It can be readied quickly in the morning, frees up my oven, tastes outstanding and can feed a crowd. Covered with colorful pineapple slices, cherries and orange glaze, its showstopping appearance appeals to both children and adults.

>   2 cans (20 ounces *each*) sliced pineapple
>   1 fully cooked boneless ham (about 6 pounds),
>   halved
>   1 jar (6 ounces) maraschino cherries, well
>   drained
>   1 jar (12 ounces) orange marmalade

Drain pineapple, reserving juice; set juice aside. Place half of the pineapple in an ungreased 5-qt. slow cooker. Top with the ham. Add cherries, remaining pineapple and reserved pineapple juice. Spoon marmalade over ham. Cover and cook on low for 6-7 hours or until heated through.

Remove to a warm serving platter. Let stand for 10-15 minutes before slicing. Serve the pineapple and cherries with the sliced ham. **Yield:** 18-20 servings.

Sesame Pork Ribs

Sesame Pork Ribs

(Pictured above)

Cook Time: 5 to 6 Hours

Sandy Alexander, Fayetteville, North Carolina

No one ever believes how little effort it takes to make these tasty tempting ribs. The flavor of the lightly sweet and tangy sauce penetrates through the meat as the ribs simmer in the slow cooker.

   3/4 cup packed brown sugar
   1/2 cup soy sauce
   1/2 cup ketchup
   1/4 cup honey
     2 tablespoons white wine vinegar *or* cider
       vinegar
     3 garlic cloves, minced
     1 teaspoon ground ginger
     1 teaspoon salt
   1/4 to 1/2 teaspoon crushed red pepper flakes
     5 pounds country-style pork ribs
     1 medium onion, sliced
     2 tablespoons sesame seeds, toasted
     2 tablespoons chopped green onions

In a large bowl, combine the first nine ingredients. Add ribs and turn to coat. Place onion in a 5-qt. slow cooker; arrange ribs on top and pour sauce over. Cover and cook on low for 5-6 hours or until a meat thermometer reads 160°-170°. Place ribs on a serving platter; sprinkle with sesame seeds and green onions. **Yield:** 6 servings.

Pork Chops and Beans

Cook Time: 8 to 9-1/2 Hours

Dorothy Pritchett, Wills Point, Texas

This hearty combination of juicy pork chops and two kinds of beans makes a satisfying supper from the slow cooker in summer or winter.

     4 pork loin chops (1/2 inch thick)
   1/2 teaspoon salt
   1/4 teaspoon pepper
     1 tablespoon vegetable oil
     2 medium onions, chopped
     2 garlic cloves, minced
   1/4 cup chili sauce
1-1/2 teaspoons brown sugar
     1 teaspoon prepared mustard
     1 can (16 ounces) kidney beans, rinsed and
       drained
     1 can (15-1/4 ounces) lima beans, rinsed and
       drained *or* 1-3/4 cups frozen lima beans

Sprinkle pork chops with salt and pepper. In a skillet, brown chops in oil; transfer chops to a slow cooker. Reserve 1 tablespoon drippings in the skillet; saute onions and garlic until tender. Stir in chili sauce, brown sugar and mustard. Pour over chops. Cover and cook on low for 7-8 hours. Stir in beans. Cover and cook 1 to 1-1/2 hours longer or until meat juices run clear and beans are heated through. **Yield:** 4 servings.

Polish Kraut and Apples

(Pictured below)

Cook Time: 4 to 5 Hours

Caren Markee, Cary, Illinois

My family loves this hearty heartwarming meal on cold winter nights. The tender apples, brown sugar and smoked sausage give this dish fantastic flavor. I like making it because the prep time is very short.

- 1 can (14 ounces) sauerkraut, rinsed and well drained
- 1 pound fully cooked Polish sausage *or* kielbasa, cut into 2-inch pieces
- 3 medium tart apples, peeled and cut into eighths
- 1/2 cup packed brown sugar
- 1/2 teaspoon caraway seed, optional
- 1/8 teaspoon pepper
- 3/4 cup apple juice

Place half of the sauerkraut in an ungreased slow cooker. Top with sausage, apples, brown sugar, caraway seed if desired and pepper. Top with remaining sauerkraut. Pour apple juice over all. Cover and cook on low for 4-5 hours or until apples are tender. **Yield:** 4 servings.

Ham and Hash Browns

Cook Time: 7 to 8 Hours

Marlene Muckenhirn, Delano, Minnesota

You just can't beat the slow cooker for convenience…I use mine two or three times a week all year-round. Here's a new way to prepare an old-fashioned favorite.

Polish Kraut and Apples

- 1 package (28 ounces) frozen O'Brien hash brown potatoes
- 2 cups cubed fully cooked ham
- 1 jar (2 ounces) diced pimientos, drained
- 1 can (10-3/4 ounces) condensed cheddar cheese soup, undiluted
- 3/4 cup milk
- 1/4 teaspoon pepper

In a slow cooker, combine potatoes, ham and pimientos. In a bowl, combine soup, milk and pepper; pour over potato mixture. Cover and cook on low for 7-8 hours or until potatoes are tender. **Yield:** 4 servings.

San Francisco Chops

Cook Time: 7-1/2 to 8-1/2 Hours

Tara Bonesteel, Dayton, New Jersey

It's easy to please friends and family with these fast-to-fix chops. Simmered in a tangy sauce all day, they're so moist and delicious by dinnertime they practically melt in your mouth.

- 4 bone-in pork loin chops (1 inch thick)
- 1 to 2 tablespoons vegetable oil
- 1 garlic clove, minced
- 1/4 cup soy sauce
- 1/4 cup red wine *or* chicken broth
- 2 tablespoons brown sugar
- 1/4 teaspoon crushed red pepper flakes
- 1 tablespoon cornstarch
- 1 tablespoon cold water

Hot cooked rice

In a skillet, brown pork chops on both sides in oil; transfer to a slow cooker. Add garlic to drippings; cook and stir for about 1 minute or until golden. Stir in soy sauce, wine or broth, brown sugar and red pepper flakes; cook and stir until sugar is dissolved. Pour over chops. Cover and cook on low for 7-8 hours or until meat is tender.

Remove chops. Combine cornstarch and cold water until smooth; gradually stir into slow cooker. Return chops to slow cooker. Cover and cook for at least 30 minutes or until slightly thickened. Serve over rice. **Yield:** 4 servings.

Cranberry Pork Chops

Cook Time: 7 to 8 Hours

Robin Czachor, Appleton, Wisconsin

My family raves over these chops. Use the mild sweet-and-sour sauce to make a gravy for mashed potatoes. Add a salad and you have a great meal that didn't keep you in the kitchen for hours.

- 6 bone-in pork loin chops
- 1 can (16 ounces) jellied cranberry sauce
- 1/2 cup cranberry *or* apple juice
- 1/4 cup sugar
- 2 tablespoons spicy brown mustard
- 2 tablespoons cornstarch
- 1/4 cup cold water
- 1/2 teaspoon salt

Dash pepper

Teriyaki Pork Roast

Herb-Stuffed Chops

(Pictured below)

Cook Time: 8 to 9 Hours

Diane Seeger, New Springfield, Ohio

Guests will think you stayed home all day when you serve these tender stuffed chops. I often share this recipe with new brides because I know it will become one of their favorites.

>   3/4 cup chopped onion
>   1/4 cup chopped celery
>   2 tablespoons butter *or* margarine
>   2 cups day-old bread cubes
>   1/2 cup minced fresh parsley
>   1/3 cup evaporated milk
>   1 teaspoon fennel seed, crushed
>   1-1/2 teaspoons salt, *divided*
>   1/2 teaspoon pepper, *divided*
>   6 rib *or* loin pork chops (1 inch thick)
>   1 tablespoon vegetable oil
>   3/4 cup white wine *or* chicken broth

In a skillet, saute onion and celery in butter until tender. Add bread cubes, parsley, milk, fennel, 1/4 teaspoon salt and 1/8 teaspoon pepper; toss to coat. Cut a pocket in each chop by slicing from the fat side almost to the bone. Spoon about 1/4 cup stuffing into each pocket. Combine the remaining salt and pepper; rub over chops. In a skillet, brown the chops in oil; transfer to a slow cooker. Pour wine or broth over the chops. Cover and cook on low for 8-9 hours or until meat juices run clear. **Yield:** 6 servings.

Place pork chops in a slow cooker. Combine the cranberry sauce, juice, sugar and mustard until smooth; pour over chops. Cover and cook on low for 7-8 hours or until the meat is tender. Remove chops; keep warm.

In a saucepan, combine the cornstarch and cold water until smooth; gradually stir in cooking juices. Bring to a boil; cook and stir for 2 minutes or until thickened. Stir in salt and pepper. Serve over chops. **Yield:** 6 servings.

Teriyaki Pork Roast

(Pictured above)

Cook Time: 7 to 8 Hours

Roxanne Hulsey, Gainesville, Georgia

Since my husband works full-time and attends school, I do a great deal around the house. I'm always looking for no-fuss recipes, so I was thrilled to find this one. The moist teriyaki-seasoned pork roast has become a family favorite.

>   3/4 cup unsweetened apple juice
>   2 tablespoons sugar
>   2 tablespoons soy sauce
>   1 tablespoon vinegar
>   1 teaspoon ground ginger
>   1/4 teaspoon garlic powder
>   1/8 teaspoon pepper
>   1 boneless pork loin roast (about 3 pounds),
>   halved
>   7-1/2 teaspoons cornstarch
>   3 tablespoons cold water

Combine the first seven ingredients in a greased slow cooker. Add roast and turn to coat. Cover and cook on low for 7-8 hours or until a thermometer inserted into the roast reads 160°. Remove roast and keep warm. In a saucepan, combine cornstarch and cold water until smooth; stir in cooking juices. Bring to a boil; cook and stir for 2 minutes or until thickened. Serve with the roast. **Yield:** 8 servings.

Herb-Stuffed Chops

Side Dishes & Condiments

Slow-Cooked Broccoli (p. 99)

Chapter 7

Michigan Beans and Sausage

Michigan Beans and Sausage

(Pictured above)

Cook Time: 6 to 8 Hours

Janice Lass, Dorr, Michigan

This recipe from a church cookbook caught my eye years ago. Bean casseroles are a big hit at potlucks and picnics.

> 1 pound fully cooked kielbasa *or* Polish sausage, halved lengthwise and thinly sliced
> 1 medium onion, chopped
> 1 cup ketchup
> 3/4 cup packed brown sugar
> 1/2 cup sugar
> 2 tablespoons vinegar
> 2 tablespoons molasses
> 2 tablespoons prepared mustard
> 3 cans (15-1/2 ounces *each*) great northern beans, rinsed and drained

In a saucepan, cook sausage and onion in boiling water for 2 minutes; drain. In a bowl, combine the ketchup, sugars, vinegar, molasses and mustard. Stir in the beans and sausage mixture. Transfer to a slow cooker. Cover and cook on low for 6-8 hours or until heated through. **Yield:** 14-16 servings.

Cheesy Spinach

Cook Time: 5 to 6 Hours

Frances Moore, Decatur, Illinois

My daughter often serves this cheese and spinach blend at church suppers. She always comes home with an empty slow cooker. Everyone likes this flavorful treatment once they try it.

> 2 packages (10 ounces *each*) frozen chopped spinach, thawed and well drained

> 2 cups (16 ounces) small-curd cottage cheese
> 1-1/2 cups cubed process American cheese
> 3 eggs, lightly beaten
> 1/4 cup butter *or* margarine, cubed
> 1/4 cup all-purpose flour
> 1 teaspoon salt

In a large bowl, combine all ingredients. Pour into a greased slow cooker. Cover and cook on high for 1 hour. Reduce heat to low; cook 4-5 hours longer or until a knife inserted near the center comes out clean. **Yield:** 6-8 servings.

Spanish Hominy

Cook Time: 6 to 8 Hours

Donna Brockett, Kingfisher, Oklahoma

I received this recipe from a good friend who is known to be a fabulous cook. The colorful side dish gets its zesty flavor from spicy canned tomatoes with green chilies. It's a great way to perk up any main dish.

> 4 cans (15-1/2 ounces *each*) hominy, drained
> 1 can (14-1/2 ounces) diced tomatoes, undrained
> 1 can (10 ounces) diced tomatoes and green chilies, undrained
> 1 can (8 ounces) tomato sauce
> 3/4 pound sliced bacon, diced
> 1 large onion, chopped
> 1 medium green pepper, chopped

In a slow cooker, combine the hominy, tomatoes and tomato sauce. In a skillet, cook the bacon until crisp; remove with a slotted spoon to paper towels. Drain, reserving 1 tablespoon drippings.

Saute the onion and green pepper in the drippings until tender. Stir the onion mixture and bacon into the hominy mixture. Cover and cook on low for 6-8 hours or until heated through. **Yield:** 12 servings.

Four-Bean Medley

Cook Time: 6 to 7 Hours

Susanne Wasson, Montgomery, New York

This bean side dish always draws compliments. It's a hearty and great-tasting complement to any meal. Because it's easy to fix ahead and simmer in the slow cooker, it's convenient to take to potluck dinners and church meals.

> 8 bacon strips, diced
> 2 medium onions, quartered and sliced
> 3/4 cup packed brown sugar
> 1/2 cup vinegar
> 1 teaspoon salt
> 1 teaspoon ground mustard
> 1/2 teaspoon garlic powder
> 1 can (16 ounces) baked beans, undrained
> 1 can (16 ounces) kidney beans, rinsed and drained
> 1 can (15-1/2 ounces) butter beans, rinsed and drained
> 1 can (14-1/2 ounces) cut green beans, drained

In a skillet, cook bacon until crisp. Drain, reserving 2 tablespoons drippings; set bacon aside. Saute onions in drippings until tender. Stir in brown sugar, vinegar, salt, mustard and garlic powder. Simmer, uncovered, for 15 minutes or until the onions are golden brown.

Combine the beans in a slow cooker. Add onion mixture and bacon; mix well. Cover and cook on low for 6-7 hours or until the beans are tender. Serve with a slotted spoon. **Yield:** 8-10 servings.

Cheesy Creamed Corn

(Pictured below)

Cook Time: 4 Hours

Mary Ann Truit, Wichita, Kansas

My family really likes this creamy, cheesy side dish—and it's so easy to make. Even those who usually don't eat much corn will ask for a second helping.

- 3 packages (16 ounces *each*) frozen corn
- 2 packages (one 8 ounces, one 3 ounces) cream cheese, cubed
- 1/4 cup butter *or* margarine, cubed
- 3 tablespoons water
- 3 tablespoons milk
- 2 tablespoons sugar
- 6 slices process American cheese, cut into small pieces

Combine all ingredients in a slow cooker; mix well. Cover and cook on low for 4 hours or until heated through and the cheese is melted. Stir well before serving. **Yield:** 12 servings.

Lemon Red Potatoes

(Pictured below)

Cook Time: 2-1/2 to 3 Hours

Tara Branham, Cedar Park, Texas

Butter, lemon juice, parsley and chives enhance simple red potatoes. Since they cook in the slow cooker, there's plenty of room on the stove for other dishes.

- 1-1/2 pounds medium red potatoes
- 1/4 cup water
- 1/4 cup butter *or* margarine, melted
- 1 tablespoon lemon juice
- 3 tablespoons snipped fresh parsley
- 1 tablespoon snipped fresh chives

Salt and pepper to taste

Cut a strip of peel from around the middle of each potato. Place potatoes and water in a slow cooker. Cover and cook on high for 2-1/2 to 3 hours or until tender (do not overcook); drain. Combine butter, lemon juice, parsley and chives; mix well. Pour over the potatoes and toss to coat. Season with salt and pepper. **Yield:** 6 servings.

Lemon Red Potatoes
Cheesy Creamed Corn

Slow-Cooked Mac 'n' Cheese

Simple Saucy Potatoes

Cook Time: 4 to 5 Hours

Gloria Schroeder, Ottawa Lake, Michigan

These rich and creamy potatoes are easy to prepare for potlucks and holiday meals. This saucy side dish always gets rave reviews wherever I take it.

- **4 cans (15 ounces *each*) sliced white potatoes, drained**
- **2 cans (10-3/4 ounces *each*) condensed cream of celery soup, undiluted**
- **2 cups (16 ounces) sour cream**
- **10 bacon strips, cooked and crumbled**
- **6 green onions, thinly sliced**

Place potatoes in a slow cooker. Combine the remaining ingredients; pour over potatoes and mix well. Cover and cook on high for 4-5 hours. **Yield:** 12 servings.

All-Day Apple Butter

Cook Time: 11 to 13 Hours

Betty Ruenholl, Syracuse, Nebraska

I make several batches of this simple and delicious apple butter to freeze in jars. Depending on the sweetness of the apples used, you can adjust the sugar to taste. With this spread, the fresh flavor of apples at harvesttime can be enjoyed all year.

- **5-1/2 pounds apples, peeled and finely chopped**
- **4 cups sugar**
- **2 to 3 teaspoons ground cinnamon**

- **1/4 teaspoon ground cloves**
- **1/4 teaspoon salt**

Place apples in a slow cooker. Combine sugar, cinnamon, cloves and salt; pour over apples and mix well. Cover and cook on high for 1 hour. Reduce heat to low; cover and cook for 9-11 hours or until thickened and dark brown, stirring occasionally (stir more frequently as it thickens to prevent sticking).

Uncover and cook on low 1 hour longer. If desired, stir with a wire whisk until smooth. Spoon into freezer containers, leaving 1/2-in. headspace. Cover and refrigerate or freeze. **Yield:** 4 pints.

Slow-Cooked Mac 'n' Cheese

(Pictured at left)

Cook Time: 4-1/2 Hours

Bernice Glascoe, Roxboro, North Carolina

This cheesy classic casserole is a great way to spark satisfied smiles around the table. It's homespun comfort food that goes well with any meat and is even rich and filling enough to be the entree.

- **1 package (16 ounces) elbow macaroni**
- **1/2 cup butter *or* margarine, melted**
- **2 eggs, beaten**
- **1 can (12 ounces) evaporated milk**
- **1 can (10-3/4 ounces) condensed cheddar cheese soup, undiluted**
- **1 cup milk**
- **4 cups (16 ounces) shredded cheddar cheese, *divided***
- **1/8 teaspoon paprika**

Cook macaroni according to package directions; drain. Place in a 5-qt. slow cooker; add butter. In a bowl, combine the eggs, evaporated milk, soup, milk and 3 cups cheese. Pour over macaroni mixture; stir to combine. Cover and cook on low for 4 hours. Sprinkle with the remaining cheese. Cook 15 minutes longer or until cheese is melted. Sprinkle with paprika. **Yield:** 10 servings.

Slow-Cooked Sage Dressing

Cook Time: 4 to 5 Hours

Ellen Benninger, Stoneboro, Pennsylvania

This recipe is such a help when I'm fixing a big holiday meal. There's room in the oven for other dishes when this simple yet delicious dressing is fixed in the slow cooker.

- **14 to 15 cups day-old bread cubes**
- **3 cups chopped celery**
- **1-1/2 cups chopped onion**
- **1-1/2 teaspoons rubbed sage**
- **1 teaspoon salt**
- **1/2 teaspoon pepper**
- **1-1/4 cups butter *or* margarine, melted**

Combine bread, celery, onion, sage, salt and pepper; mix well. Add butter and toss. Spoon into a 5-qt. slow cooker. Cover and cook on low for 4-5 hours, stirring once. **Yield:** about 12 servings.

Slow-Simmered Kidney Beans

(Pictured below)

Cook Time: 6 to 8 Hours

Sheila Vail, Long Beach, California

My husband always puts us down for this side dish when we're invited to a potluck. Canned beans cut down on prep time yet get plenty of zip from bacon, apple, red pepper and onion. I like simmering this mixture in the slow cooker because it blends the flavors, and I don't have to stand over the stove.

- 6 bacon strips, diced
- 1/2 pound fully cooked Polish sausage *or* kielbasa, chopped
- 4 cans (16 ounces *each*) kidney beans, rinsed and drained
- 1 can (28 ounces) diced tomatoes, drained
- 2 medium sweet red peppers, chopped
- 1 large onion, chopped
- 1 cup ketchup
- 1/2 cup packed brown sugar
- 1/4 cup honey
- 1/4 cup molasses
- 1 tablespoon Worcestershire sauce
- 1 teaspoon salt
- 1 teaspoon ground mustard
- 2 medium unpeeled red apples, cored and cut into 1/2-inch pieces

In a skillet, cook bacon until crisp. Remove with a slotted spoon to paper towels. Add sausage to drippings; cook and stir 5 minutes. Drain; set aside.

In an ungreased 5-qt. slow cooker, combine the beans, tomatoes, red peppers, onion, ketchup, brown sugar, honey, molasses, Worcestershire sauce,

Slow-Simmered Kidney Beans

Creamy Hash Browns

salt and mustard. Stir in the bacon and sausage. Cover and cook on low for 4-6 hours. Stir in the apples. Cover and cook 2 hours longer or until bubbly. **Yield:** 16 servings.

Creamy Hash Browns

(Pictured above)

Cook Time: 4 to 5 Hours

Donna Downes, Las Vegas, Nevada

My mother often took this comforting side dish to social dinners because it was such a hit. Now I get the same compliments when I make it. The popular flavors of bacon and onion jazz up a creamy mixture that takes advantage of convenient frozen hash browns and canned soups.

- 1 package (2 pounds) frozen cubed hash brown potatoes
- 2 cups (8 ounces) cubed *or* shredded process American cheese
- 2 cups (16 ounces) sour cream
- 1 can (10-3/4 ounces) condensed cream of celery soup, undiluted
- 1 can (10-3/4 ounces) condensed cream of chicken soup, undiluted
- 1 pound sliced bacon, cooked and crumbled
- 1 large onion, chopped
- 1/4 cup butter *or* margarine, melted
- 1/4 teaspoon pepper

Place potatoes in an ungreased 5-qt. slow cooker. In a bowl, combine the remaining ingredients. Pour over potatoes and mix well. Cover and cook on low for 4-5 hours or until potatoes are tender and heated through. **Yield:** 14 servings.

Vegetable Medley

Vegetable Medley
(Pictured above)

Cook Time: 5 to 6 Hours

Terry Maly, Olathe, Kansas

This is a wonderful side dish to make when garden vegetables are plentiful. The colorful combination is a great complement to any entree.

      4 cups diced peeled potatoes
1-1/2 cups frozen whole kernel corn *or* 1 can
           (15-1/4 ounces) whole kernel corn, drained
      4 medium tomatoes, seeded and diced
      1 cup sliced carrots
  1/2 cup chopped onion
  3/4 teaspoon salt
  1/2 teaspoon sugar
  1/2 teaspoon dill weed
  1/8 teaspoon pepper

In a slow cooker, combine all ingredients. Cover and cook on low for 5-6 hours or until vegetables are tender. **Yield:** 8 servings.

Sweet Potato Stuffing

Cook Time: 4 Hours

Kelly Pollock, London, Ontario

Mom likes to make sure there will be enough stuffing to satisfy our large family. For our holiday gatherings, she slow-cooks this tasty sweet potato dressing in addition to the traditional stuffing cooked inside the turkey.

  1/2 cup chopped celery
  1/2 cup chopped onion
  1/4 cup butter *or* margarine
      6 cups dry bread cubes
      1 large sweet potato, cooked, peeled and
           finely chopped
  1/2 cup chicken broth
  1/4 cup chopped pecans
  1/2 teaspoon poultry seasoning
  1/2 teaspoon rubbed sage
  1/2 teaspoon salt
  1/2 teaspoon pepper

In a skillet, saute celery and onion in butter until tender. Add remaining ingredients; toss gently. Transfer to a greased slow cooker. Cover and cook on low for 4 hours or until bread and vegetables are soft. **Yield:** 10 servings.

Saucy Scalloped Potatoes

Cook Time: 7 to 9 Hours

Elaine Kane, Keizer, Oregon

For old-fashioned flavor, try these scalloped potatoes. They cook up tender, creamy and comforting. Chopped ham adds a hearty touch.

      4 cups thinly sliced peeled potatoes
           (about 2 pounds)
      1 can (10-3/4 ounces) cream of celery *or*
           mushroom soup, undiluted
      1 can (12 ounces) evaporated milk
      1 large onion, sliced
      2 tablespoons butter *or* margarine
  1/2 teaspoon salt
  1/4 teaspoon pepper
1-1/2 cups chopped fully cooked ham

In a slow cooker, combine the first seven ingredients; mix well. Cover and cook on high for 1 hour. Stir in ham. Reduce heat to low; cook 6-8 hours longer or until potatoes are tender. **Yield:** 8-12 side-dish or 4-6 main-dish servings.

Hot German Potato Salad

Cook Time: 4 to 5 Hours

Marlene Muckenhirn, Delano, Minnesota

I make this zesty salad with potatoes, celery and onion. It's a terrific side dish when served warm with crumbled bacon and fresh parsley sprinkled on top.

      8 medium potatoes, peeled and cut into
           1/4-inch slices
      2 celery ribs, chopped
      1 large onion, chopped
      1 cup water
  2/3 cup cider vinegar
  1/3 cup sugar
      2 tablespoons quick-cooking tapioca
      1 teaspoon salt
  3/4 teaspoon celery seed
  1/4 teaspoon pepper
      6 bacon strips, cooked and crumbled
  1/4 cup minced fresh parsley

In a slow cooker, combine the potatoes, celery and onion. In a bowl, combine the water, vinegar, sugar, tapioca, salt, celery seed and pepper. Pour over the potatoes; stir gently to coat. Cover and cook on high for 4-5 hours or until potatoes are tender. Just before serving, sprinkle with bacon and parsley. **Yield:** 8-10 servings.

Moist Poultry Dressing

(Pictured below)

Cook Time: 4 to 5 Hours

Ruth Ann Stelfox, Raymond, Alberta

Tasty mushrooms and onions complement the big herb flavor in this dressing. Every forkful stays wonderfully moist when cooked this way.

        2 jars (4-1/2 ounces *each*) sliced mushrooms, drained
        4 celery ribs, chopped
        2 medium onions, chopped
    1/4 cup minced fresh parsley
    3/4 cup butter *or* margarine
    1-1/2 pounds day-old bread, crusts removed and cubed (about 13 cups)
    1-1/2 teaspoons salt
    1-1/2 teaspoons rubbed sage
        1 teaspoon poultry seasoning
        1 teaspoon dried thyme
    1/2 teaspoon pepper
        2 eggs
        1 can (14-1/2 ounces) chicken broth

In a large skillet, saute the mushrooms, celery, onions and parsley in butter until the vegetables are tender. In a large bowl, toss the bread cubes with salt, sage,

Hot Fruit Salad

poultry seasoning, thyme and pepper. Add the mushroom mixture. Combine eggs and broth; add to the bread mixture and toss. Transfer to a slow cooker.

Cover and cook on low for 4-5 hours or until a meat thermometer reads 160°. **Yield:** 12-16 servings.

Hot Fruit Salad

(Pictured above)

Cook Time: 3 to 4 Hours

Barb Vande Voort, New Sharon, Iowa

This spicy fruit mixture is a breeze to make—just open the cans and empty them into the slow cooker With its pretty color from cherry pie filling, this salad is nice around the holidays…or for any special occasion.

        1 jar (25 ounces) chunky applesauce
        1 can (21 ounces) cherry pie filling
        1 can (20 ounces) pineapple chunks, undrained
        1 can (15-1/4 ounces) sliced peaches, undrained
        1 can (15-1/4 ounces) apricot halves, undrained
        1 can (15 ounces) mandarin oranges, undrained
    1/2 cup packed brown sugar
        1 teaspoon ground cinnamon

Place the first six ingredients in a slow cooker and stir gently. Combine brown sugar and cinnamon; sprinkle over fruit mixture. Cover and cook on low for 3-4 hours. **Yield:** 16 servings.

Moist Poultry Dressing

Broth or Bouillon?

Broth and bouillon are interchangeable. Broth is quicker, since it's ready to pour. However, one bouillon cube or 1 teaspoon of granules dissolved in 1 cup of boiling water may be substituted for 1 cup of broth in any recipe.

Slow Cooker Mashed Potatoes

2 cans (10-3/4 ounces *each*) condensed
   cheddar cheese soup, undiluted
1-1/3 cups buttermilk
2 tablespoons butter *or* margarine, melted
1/2 teaspoon seasoned salt
1/4 teaspoon garlic powder
1/4 teaspoon pepper
1 package (2 pounds) frozen cubed hash
   brown potatoes
1/4 cup grated Parmesan cheese
1 teaspoon paprika

In a slow cooker, combine the first six ingredients; stir in hash browns. Sprinkle with Parmesan cheese and paprika. Cover and cook on low for 4 to 4-1/2 hours or until potatoes are tender. **Yield:** 6-8 servings.

Chunky Applesauce

(Pictured below)

Cook Time: 6 to 8 Hours

Lisa Roessner, Ft. Recovery, Ohio

I'm so glad my mother gave me the recipe for this warm and cinnamony apple dish. Simmering it in a slow cooker fills the house with a wonderful aroma. I sometimes also serve it with cream for dessert.

8 to 10 large tart apples, peeled and cut into
   chunks
1/2 to 1 cup sugar
1/2 cup water
1 teaspoon ground cinnamon

Combine apples, sugar, water and cinnamon in a 3-qt. slow cooker; stir gently. Cover and cook on low for 6-8 hours or until apples are tender. **Yield:** 5 cups.

Slow Cooker Mashed Potatoes

(Pictured above)

Cook Time: 2 to 4 Hours

Trudy Vincent, Valles Mines, Missouri

Sour cream and cream cheese give richness to these smooth make-ahead potatoes. They are wonderful for Thanksgiving or Christmas dinner, since there's no last-minute mashing required.

1 package (3 ounces) cream cheese, softened
1/2 cup sour cream
1/4 cup butter *or* margarine, softened
1 envelope ranch salad dressing mix
1 teaspoon dried parsley flakes
6 cups warm mashed potatoes (prepared
   without milk or butter)

In a bowl, combine the cream cheese, sour cream, butter, salad dressing mix and parsley; stir in potatoes. Transfer to a slow cooker. Cover and cook on low for 2-4 hours. **Yield:** 8-10 servings.

   Editor's Note: This recipe was tested with fresh potatoes (not instant) in a slow cooker with heating elements surrounding the unit, not only in the base.

Cheesy Hash Brown Potatoes

Cook Time: 4 to 4-1/2 Hours

Becky Weseman, Becker, Minnesota

I adapted this recipe for my slow cooker, so I could bring these cheesy potatoes to a potluck picnic. Canned soup and frozen hash browns make this dish easy to assemble.

Chunky Applesauce

Side Dishes & Condiments

Lazy-Day Cranberry Relish

Cook Time: 6 Hours

June Formanek, Belle Plaine, Iowa

When I get busy with holiday bustle, this no-fuss, ruby-red condiment can be simmering in my kitchen. It's especially delicious served alongside turkey.

2 cups sugar
1 cup orange juice
1 teaspoon grated orange peel
4 cups fresh *or* frozen cranberries

In a slow cooker, combine sugar, orange juice and peel; stir until sugar is dissolved. Add the cranberries. Cover and cook on low for 6 hours. Mash the mixture. Chill several hours or overnight. **Yield:** 10-12 servings (3 cups).

Spiced Acorn Squash

Cook Time: 4 Hours

Carol Greco, Centereach, New York

Working full-time, I found I didn't always have time to cook the meals my family loved. So I re-created many of our favorites in the slow cooker. This cinnamony treatment for squash is one of them.

3/4 cup packed brown sugar
1 teaspoon ground cinnamon
1 teaspoon ground nutmeg
2 small acorn squash, halved and seeded
3/4 cup raisins
4 tablespoons butter *or* margarine
1/2 cup water

Combine brown sugar, cinnamon and nutmeg; spoon into the squash halves. Sprinkle with raisins. Top each with 1 tablespoon of butter. Wrap each squash half individually in heavy-duty foil; seal tightly. Pour water into a slow cooker. Place the squash, cut side up, in slow cooker (packets may be stacked). Cover and cook on high for 4 hours or until the squash is tender. Open foil packets carefully to allow steam to escape. **Yield:** 4 servings.

Creamy Red Potatoes

Cook Time: 8 Hours

Sheila Schmitt, Topeka, Kansas

I can please a crowd with this rich and creamy potato side dish. It's easy to double, and I always receive compliments when I take it to potlucks.

2 pounds small red potatoes, quartered
1 package (8 ounces) cream cheese, softened
1 can (10-3/4 ounces) condensed cream of potato soup, undiluted
1 envelope ranch salad dressing mix

Place potatoes in a slow cooker. In a small mixing bowl, beat cream cheese, soup and salad dressing mix until blended. Stir into potatoes. Cover and cook on low for 8 hours or until potatoes are tender. **Yield:** 4-6 servings.

Partytime Beans

Partytime Beans

(Pictured above)

Cook Time: 5 to 7 Hours

Jean Cantner, Boston, Virginia

A friend brought this colorful bean dish to my house for a church circle potluck dinner. As soon as I tasted these slightly sweet baked beans, I had to have the recipe. I've served this and shared the recipe many times since.

1-1/2 cups ketchup
1 medium onion, chopped
1 medium green pepper, chopped
1 medium sweet red pepper, chopped
1/2 cup water
1/2 cup packed brown sugar
2 bay leaves
2 to 3 teaspoons cider vinegar
1 teaspoon ground mustard
1/8 teaspoon pepper
1 can (16 ounces) kidney beans, rinsed and drained
1 can (15-1/2 ounces) great northern beans, rinsed and drained
1 can (15 ounces) lima beans, rinsed and drained
1 can (15 ounces) black beans, rinsed and drained
1 can (15-1/2 ounces) black-eyed peas, rinsed and drained

In a slow cooker, combine the first 10 ingredients; mix well. Add the beans and peas; mix well. Cover and cook on low for 5-7 hours or until onion and peppers are tender. Remove bay leaves. **Yield:** 14-16 servings.

Sweet 'n' Sour Beans

pings. In the drippings, saute onions until tender. Add brown sugar, vinegar, salt, mustard and garlic powder. Bring to a boil. In a slow cooker, combine beans and peas. Add onion mixture and bacon; mix well. Cover and cook on high for 3-4 hours or until heated through. **Yield:** 15-20 servings.

Slow-Cooked Vegetables

Cook Time: 7 to 8 Hours

Kathy Westendorf, Westgate, Iowa

I simmer an assortment of garden-fresh vegetables into this satisfying side dish. My sister-in-law shared this recipe with me. It's a favorite at holiday gatherings and potlucks.

        4 celery ribs, cut into 1-inch pieces
        4 small carrots, cut into 1-inch pieces
        2 medium tomatoes, cut into chunks
        2 medium onions, thinly sliced
        2 cups cut fresh green beans (1-inch pieces)
        1 medium green pepper, cut into 1-inch pieces
    1/4 cup butter *or* margarine, melted
        3 tablespoons quick-cooking tapioca
        1 tablespoon sugar
        2 teaspoons salt
    1/8 teaspoon pepper

Place the vegetables in a slow cooker. Combine butter, tapioca, sugar, salt and pepper; pour over vegetables and stir well. Cover and cook on low for 7-8 hours or until vegetables are tender. Serve with a slotted spoon. **Yield:** 8 servings.

Sweet 'n' Sour Beans

(Pictured above)

Cook Time: 3 to 4 Hours

Barbara Short, Mena, Arkansas

This recipe is popular on both sides of the border. It came from a friend in Alaska, then traveled with me to Mexico, where I lived for 5 years, and is now a potluck favorite in my Arkansas community. It's easy to keep the beans warm and serve from a slow cooker.

        8 bacon strips, diced
        2 medium onions, halved and thinly sliced
        1 cup packed brown sugar
    1/2 cup cider vinegar
        1 teaspoon salt
        1 teaspoon ground mustard
    1/2 teaspoon garlic powder
        1 can (28 ounces) baked beans, undrained
        1 can (16 ounces) kidney beans, rinsed and drained
        1 can (15-1/2 ounces) pinto beans, rinsed and drained
        1 can (15 ounces) lima beans, rinsed and drained
        1 can (15-1/2 ounces) black-eyed peas, rinsed and drained

In a large skillet, cook bacon until crisp. Remove to paper towels. Drain, reserving 2 tablespoons drip-

Potato Hot Dish

Cook Time: 8 to 10 Hours

Melissa Marzolf, Marysville, Michigan

For a comforting side dish that feeds a crowd, try these saucy slow-cooked potatoes. A simple topping of buttered croutons covers the creamy combination.

        6 medium potatoes, peeled and cut into 1/4-inch strips
        2 cups (8 ounces) shredded cheddar cheese
        1 can (10-3/4 ounces) condensed cream of chicken soup, undiluted
        1 small onion, chopped *or* 1 tablespoon dried minced onion
        7 tablespoons butter *or* margarine, melted, *divided*

Better Safe Than Sorry

If you're not home during the entire slow-cooking process and there was a power outage, for food-safety reasons, it's best to throw away the food in your slow cooker even if it looks done.

1 teaspoon salt
1 teaspoon pepper
1 cup (8 ounces) sour cream
2 cups seasoned stuffing cubes

Toss the potatoes and cheese; place in a 5-qt. slow cooker. Combine soup, onion, 4 tablespoons butter, salt and pepper; pour over potato mixture. Cover and cook on low for 8-10 hours or until potatoes are tender. Stir in sour cream. Toss stuffing cubes and remaining butter; sprinkle over potatoes. **Yield:** 10-12 servings.

Pineapple Sweet Potatoes

Cook Time: 4 to 5 Hours

Bette Fulcher, Lexington, Texas

Pineapple and pecans make a pretty topping for this no-fuss fall side dish. It's light, tasty and not too sweet. Making it in the slow cooker leaves extra space in the oven when preparing a holiday turkey and other dishes.

6 to 6-1/2 cups mashed sweet potatoes
   (without added milk or butter)
4 eggs
1 cup milk
1/2 cup butter *or* margarine, softened
1 teaspoon vanilla extract
1/2 teaspoon lemon extract
1 teaspoon salt
1 teaspoon ground cinnamon
1/2 teaspoon ground nutmeg
1 can (8 ounces) pineapple slices, drained
1/4 cup chopped pecans

In a mixing bowl, combine the first nine ingredients; mix well. Transfer to a slow cooker. Top with pineapple slices and pecans. Cover and cook on low for 4-5 hours or until a thermometer reads 160°. **Yield:** 12-14 servings.

Mushroom Wild Rice

Cook Time: 7 to 8 Hours

Bob Malchow, Monon, Indiana

This is one of my favorite recipes from my mother. With only seven ingredients, it's quick to assemble in the morning before I leave for work. By the time I get home, mouth-watering aromas have filled the house.

2-1/4 cups water
1 can (10-1/2 ounces) condensed beef
   consomme, undiluted
1 can (10-1/2 ounces) condensed French onion
   soup, undiluted
3 cans (4 ounces *each*) mushroom stems and
   pieces, drained
1/2 cup butter *or* margarine, melted
1 cup uncooked brown rice
1 cup uncooked wild rice

In a slow cooker, combine all ingredients; stir well. Cover and cook on low for 7-8 hours or until rice is tender. **Yield:** 12-16 servings.

Slow-Cooked Broccoli

(Pictured below and on page 88)

Cook Time: 2-1/2 to 3 Hours

Connie Slocum, St. Simons Island, Georgia

This casserole is quick to assemble and full of good flavor. Even those who don't usually like broccoli enjoy it served this way. I can even serve this dish in the summer alongside grilled meat, since it doesn't heat up the house as it cooks.

2 packages (10 ounces *each*) frozen chopped
   broccoli, partially thawed
1 can (10-3/4 ounces) condensed cream of
   celery soup, undiluted
1-1/2 cups (6 ounces) shredded sharp cheddar
   cheese, *divided*
1/4 cup chopped onion
1/2 teaspoon Worcestershire sauce
1/4 teaspoon pepper
1 cup crushed butter-flavored crackers
   (about 25)
2 tablespoons butter *or* margarine

In a large bowl, combine the broccoli, soup, 1 cup cheese, onion, Worcestershire sauce and pepper. Pour into a greased slow cooker. Sprinkle crackers on top; dot with butter. Cover and cook on high for 2-1/2 to 3 hours. Sprinkle with remaining cheese. Cook 10 minutes longer or until the cheese is melted. **Yield:** 8-10 servings.

Slow-Cooked Broccoli

Sweet Endings

Black and Blue Cobbler (p. 106)

Chapter 8

Pumpkin Pie Pudding

(Pictured below)

Cook Time: 6 to 7 Hours

Andrea Schaak, Bloomington, Minnesota

My husband loves anything pumpkin, and this creamy, comforting dessert is one of his favorites. We make this super-easy pudding year-round, but it's especially nice in fall.

- 1 can (15 ounces) solid-pack pumpkin
- 1 can (12 ounces) evaporated milk
- 3/4 cup sugar
- 1/2 cup biscuit/baking mix
- 2 eggs, beaten
- 2 tablespoons butter *or* margarine, melted
- 2-1/2 teaspoons pumpkin pie spice
- 2 teaspoons vanilla extract
- Whipped topping, optional

In a large bowl, combine the first eight ingredients. Transfer to a slow cooker coated with nonstick cooking spray. Cover and cook on low for 6-7 hours or until a thermometer reads 160°. Serve in bowls with whipped topping if desired. **Yield:** 6-8 servings.

Slow Cooker Bread Pudding

Cook Time: 3 Hours

Edna Hoffman, Hebron, Indiana

Use a slow cooker to turn day-old cinnamon rolls into a comforting, old-fashioned dessert. It tastes wonderful topped with lemon or vanilla sauce or whipped cream.

- 8 cups cubed day-old unfrosted cinnamon rolls*
- 2 cups milk

Pumpkin Pie Pudding

- 4 eggs
- 1/4 cup sugar
- 1/4 cup butter *or* margarine, melted
- 1/2 teaspoon vanilla extract
- 1/4 teaspoon ground nutmeg
- 1 cup raisins

Place cubed cinnamon rolls in a slow cooker. In a mixing bowl, combine the next six ingredients; beat until smooth. Stir in raisins. Pour over cinnamon rolls; stir gently. Cover and cook on low for 3 hours. **Yield:** 6 servings.

*Editor's Note: 8 slices of cinnamon or white bread, cut into 1-inch cubes, may be substituted for the cinnamon rolls.

Apple Granola Dessert

Cook Time: 6 to 8 Hours

Janis Lawrence, Childress, Texas

I would be lost without my slow cooker. Besides using it to prepare our evening meal, I often make desserts in it, including these tender apples, which get a tasty treatment from granola cereal.

- 4 medium tart apples, peeled and sliced
- 2 cups granola cereal with fruit and nuts
- 1/4 cup honey
- 2 tablespoons butter *or* margarine, melted
- 1 teaspoon ground cinnamon
- 1/2 teaspoon ground nutmeg
- Vanilla ice cream *or* whipped topping, optional

In a slow cooker, combine apples and cereal. In a bowl, combine honey, butter, cinnamon and nutmeg; pour over apple mixture and mix well. Cover and cook on low for 6-8 hours. Serve with ice cream or whipped topping if desired. **Yield:** 4-6 servings.

Fruit Compote Dessert

Cook Time: 3 to 4 Hours

Laura Bryant German, West Warren, Massachusetts

This is one of the first desserts I learned to make in the slow cooker, and it's the one guests still enjoy most. It tastes like it came from a fancy restaurant.

- 2 medium tart apples, peeled
- 2 medium fresh peaches, peeled and cubed
- 2 cups unsweetened pineapple chunks
- 1-1/4 cups unsweetened pineapple juice
- 1/4 cup honey
- 2 lemon slices (1/4 inch)
- 1 cinnamon stick (3-1/2 inches)
- 1 medium firm banana, thinly sliced
- Whipped cream, sliced almonds and maraschino cherries, optional

Cut apples into 1/4-in. slices and then in half; place in a slow cooker. Add the peaches, pineapple, pineapple juice, honey, lemon and cinnamon. Cover and cook on low for 3-4 hours. Just before serving, stir in banana slices. Serve with a slotted spoon if desired. Garnish with whipped cream, almonds and cherries if desired. **Yield:** 8 servings.

Nutty Apple Streusel Dessert

Easy Chocolate Clusters

Cook Time: 2 Hours

Doris Reynolds, Munds Park, Arizona

You can use this simple recipe to make a big batch of chocolate candy without a lot of fuss. I've sent these clusters to my husband's office a number of times…and passed the recipe along as well.

2 pounds white candy coating, broken into small pieces
2 cups (12 ounces) semisweet chocolate chips
1 package (4 ounces) German sweet chocolate
1 jar (24 ounces) dry roasted peanuts

In a slow cooker, combine candy coating, chocolate chips and German chocolate. Cover and cook on high for 1 hour. Reduce heat to low; cover and cook 1 hour longer or until melted, stirring every 15 minutes. Add peanuts; mix well. Drop by teaspoonfuls onto waxed paper. Let stand until set. Store at room temperature. **Yield:** 3-1/2 dozen.

Nutty Apple Streusel Dessert

(Pictured above)

Cook Time: 6 to 7 Hours

Jacki Every, Rotterdam, New York

Many people don't think of using a slow cooker to make dessert, but I like finishing up our dinner and having this hot, scrumptious apple treat waiting to be served up. I can start it in the morning and not think about it all day.

6 cups sliced peeled tart apples
1-1/4 teaspoons ground cinnamon
1/4 teaspoon ground allspice
1/4 teaspoon ground nutmeg
3/4 cup milk
2 tablespoons butter *or* margarine, softened
3/4 cup sugar
2 eggs
1 teaspoon vanilla extract
1/2 cup biscuit/baking mix

TOPPING:
1 cup biscuit/baking mix
1/3 cup packed brown sugar
3 tablespoons cold butter *or* margarine
1/2 cup sliced almonds
Ice cream *or* whipped cream, optional

In a large bowl, toss apples with cinnamon, allspice and nutmeg. Place in a greased slow cooker. In a mixing bowl, combine milk, butter, sugar, eggs, vanilla and baking mix; mix well. Spoon over apples. For topping, combine biscuit mix and brown sugar in a bowl; cut in butter until crumbly. Add almonds; sprinkle over apples. Cover and cook on low for 6-7 hours or until the apples are tender. Serve with ice cream or whipped cream if desired. **Yield:** 6-8 servings.

Strawberry Rhubarb Sauce

(Pictured below)

Cook Time: 6 to 7 Hours

Judith Waxman, Washington, D.C.

This tart and tangy fruit sauce is excellent over pound cake or ice cream. I've served the rosy-colored mixture many times and received rave reviews from friends and family.

6 cups chopped rhubarb (1/2-inch pieces)
1 cup sugar
1/2 teaspoon grated orange peel
1/2 teaspoon ground ginger
1 cinnamon stick (3 inches)
1/2 cup white grape juice
2 cups halved unsweetened strawberries
Pound cake *or* vanilla ice cream

Place rhubarb in a 3-qt. slow cooker. Combine sugar, orange peel and ginger; sprinkle over rhubarb. Add cinnamon stick and grape juice. Cover and cook on low for 5-6 hours or until rhubarb is tender. Stir in strawberries; cook 1 hour longer. Discard cinnamon stick. Serve over cake or ice cream. **Yield:** 10 servings.

Strawberry Rhubarb Sauce

Raisin Bread Pudding

(Pictured below)

Cook Time: 4 to 5 Hours

Sherry Niese, McComb, Ohio

My sister gave me the recipe for this delicious bread pudding that's dotted with raisins. It's a big hit with everyone who's tried it. A homemade vanilla sauce goes together quickly on the stovetop and is yummy drizzled over warm servings of this old-fashioned-tasting treat.

        8 slices bread, cubed
        4 eggs
        2 cups milk
        1/4 cup sugar
        1/4 cup butter *or* margarine, melted
        1/4 cup raisins
        1/2 teaspoon ground cinnamon
    SAUCE:
        2 tablespoons butter *or* margarine
        2 tablespoons all-purpose flour
        1 cup water
        3/4 cup sugar
        1 teaspoon vanilla extract

Place the bread cubes in a greased slow cooker. In a bowl, beat the eggs and milk; stir in the sugar, but-

Raisin Bread Pudding

ter, raisins and cinnamon. Pour over the bread cubes; stir. Cover and cook on high for 1 hour. Reduce heat to low; cook for 3-4 hours or until a thermometer reads 160°.

Just before serving, melt the butter in a saucepan. Stir in the flour until smooth. Gradually add the water, sugar and vanilla. Bring to a boil; cook and stir for 2 minutes or until thickened. Serve with warm bread pudding. **Yield:** 6 servings.

Hot Caramel Apples

Cook Time: 4 to 6 Hours

Pat Sparks, St. Charles, Missouri

Who ever thinks of making dessert in a slow cooker? I do! This old-time favorite goes together quickly...and it's such a treat to come home to the aroma of cinnamony baked apples just like Mom used to make.

        4 large tart apples, cored
        1/2 cup apple juice
        8 tablespoons brown sugar
        12 red-hot candies
        4 tablespoons butter *or* margarine
        8 caramels
        1/4 teaspoon ground cinnamon
    Whipped cream, optional

Peel about 3/4 in. off the top of each apple; place in a 3-qt. slow cooker. Pour juice over apples. Fill the center of each apple with 2 tablespoons of sugar, three red-hots, 1 tablespoon of butter and two caramels. Sprinkle with cinnamon. Cover and cook on low for 4-6 hours or until the apples are tender. Serve immediately with whipped cream if desired. **Yield:** 4 servings.

Chocolate Pudding Cake

Cook Time: 6 to 7 Hours

Paige Arnette, Lawrenceville, Georgia

This recipe makes a rich fudgy dessert that's a cross between pudding and cake. I like to serve this scrumptious treat warm with a scoop of vanilla ice cream. Whenever I take it to parties, everybody wants the recipe.

        1 package (18-1/4 ounces) chocolate cake mix
        1 package (3.9 ounces) instant chocolate
            pudding mix
        2 cups (16 ounces) sour cream
        4 eggs
        1 cup water
        3/4 cup vegetable oil
        1 cup (6 ounces) semisweet chocolate chips
    Whipped cream *or* ice cream, optional

In a mixing bowl, combine the first six ingredients. Beat on medium speed for 2 minutes. Stir in chocolate chips. Pour into a 5-qt. slow cooker that has been coated with nonstick cooking spray. Cover and cook on low for 6-7 hours or until a toothpick inserted near the center comes out with moist crumbs. Serve in bowls with whipped cream or ice cream if desired. **Yield:** 10-12 servings.

Fruit Dessert Topping

Chocolate-Raspberry Fondue

Serve in Slow Cooker

Heather Maxwell, Fort Riley, Kansas

You don't need a fancy fondue pot to make this melt-in-your-mouth concoction. I serve the dip in my small slow cooker. Folks love the chocolate-raspberry combination.

> 1 package (14 ounces) caramels
> 2 cups (12 ounces) semisweet chocolate chips
> 1 can (12 ounces) evaporated milk
> 1/2 cup butter (no substitutes)
> 1/2 cup seedless raspberry jam

Pound cake
Assorted fresh fruit

In a large saucepan, combine the first five ingredients. Cook over low heat until caramels, chips and butter are melted, about 15 minutes. Stir until smooth. Transfer to a small slow cooker or fondue pot. Serve warm with pound cake or fruit. **Yield:** 5 cups.

Fruit Dessert Topping

(Pictured above)

Cook Time: 3-1/2 to 4-1/2 Hours

Doris Heath, Franklin, North Carolina

You'll quickly warm up to the down-home flavor of this fruit topping. Spoon it over vanilla ice cream or slices of pound cake.

> 3 medium tart apples, peeled and sliced
> 3 medium pears, peeled and sliced
> 1 tablespoon lemon juice
> 1/2 cup packed brown sugar
> 1/2 cup maple syrup
> 1/4 cup butter *or* margarine, melted
> 1/2 cup chopped pecans

> 1/4 cup raisins
> 2 cinnamon sticks (3 inches)
> 1 tablespoon cornstarch
> 2 tablespoons cold water

Pound cake *or* ice cream

In a slow cooker, toss the apples and pears with the lemon juice. Combine the brown sugar, maple syrup and butter; pour over fruit. Stir in the pecans, raisins and cinnamon sticks. Cover and cook on low for 3-4 hours.

Combine the cornstarch and water until smooth; gradually stir into slow cooker. Cover and cook on high for 30-40 minutes or until thickened. Discard cinnamon sticks. Serve over pound cake or ice cream. **Yield:** about 6 cups.

Warm Apple Delight

Cook Time: 3 Hours

Rosemary Franta, New Ulm, Minnesota

I've handed out this recipe to more people than any other. It has a delicious nutty flavor. It's a light dessert served with plain or vanilla yogurt and can also be a fun brunch treat over pancakes or waffles.

> 8 medium tart apples (about 3-1/2 pounds), peeled and sliced
> 1/2 to 1 cup chopped pecans
> 3/4 cup butter *or* margarine, melted
> 1/3 cup sugar
> 1/4 cup old-fashioned oats
> 2 tablespoons lemon juice
> 1/4 teaspoon ground cinnamon

Combine all ingredients in a slow cooker. Cook on high for 3 hours, stirring occasionally. Serve warm with yogurt, waffles or pancakes. **Yield:** 4-6 servings.

Apple-Nut Bread Pudding

Apple-Nut Bread Pudding

(Pictured above)

Cook Time: 3 to 4 Hours

Lori Fox, Menomonee Falls, Wisconsin

Traditional bread pudding gives way to autumn's influences in this comforting dessert. I add apples and pecans to this slow-cooked recipe, then top warm servings with ice cream.

    8 slices raisin bread, cubed
    2 medium tart apples, peeled and sliced
    1 cup chopped pecans, toasted
    1 cup sugar
    1 teaspoon ground cinnamon
  1/2 teaspoon ground nutmeg
    3 eggs, lightly beaten
    2 cups half-and-half cream
  1/4 cup apple juice
  1/4 cup butter *or* margarine, melted
Vanilla ice cream

Place bread cubes, apples and pecans in a greased slow cooker. In a bowl, combine the sugar, cinnamon and nutmeg. Add the eggs, cream, apple juice and butter; mix well. Pour over bread mixture. Cover and cook on low for 3-4 hours or until a knife inserted in the center comes out clean. Serve with ice cream. **Yield:** 6-8 servings.

Minister's Delight

Cook Time: 2 to 3 Hours

Mary Ann Potte, Blue Springs, Missouri

You'll need just four ingredients to make this comforting dessert. A friend gave me this recipe. She said a local minister's wife fixed it every Sunday, so she named it accordingly.

    1 can (21 ounces) cherry *or* apple pie filling
    1 package (18-1/4 ounces) yellow cake mix
  1/2 cup butter *or* margarine, melted
  1/3 cup chopped walnuts, optional

Place pie filling in a slow cooker. Combine dry cake mix and butter (mixture will be crumbly); sprinkle over filling. Sprinkle with walnuts if desired. Cover

and cook on low for 2-3 hours. Serve in bowls. **Yield:** 10-12 servings.

Black and Blue Cobbler

(Pictured below and on page 100)

Cook Time: 2 to 2-1/2 Hours

Martha Creveling, Orlando, Florida

One day, I decided to try my favorite fruity dessert recipe in the slow cooker. It took a bit of experimenting, but the results are "berry" well worth it.

      1 cup all-purpose flour
  1-1/2 cups sugar, *divided*
      1 teaspoon baking powder
    1/4 teaspoon salt
    1/4 teaspoon ground cinnamon
    1/4 teaspoon ground nutmeg
      2 eggs, beaten
      2 tablespoons milk
      2 tablespoons vegetable oil
      2 cups fresh *or* frozen blackberries
      2 cups fresh *or* frozen blueberries
    3/4 cup water
      1 teaspoon grated orange peel
Whipped cream *or* ice cream, optional

In a bowl, combine flour, 3/4 cup sugar, baking powder, salt, cinnamon and nutmeg. Combine eggs, milk and oil; stir into dry ingredients just until moistened. Spread the batter evenly onto the bottom of a greased 5-qt. slow cooker. In a saucepan, combine berries, water, orange peel and remaining sugar; bring to a boil. Remove from the heat; immediately pour over batter.

Cover and cook on high for 2 to 2-1/2 hours or until a toothpick inserted into the batter comes out clean. Turn cooker off. Uncover and let stand for 30 minutes before serving. Serve with whipped cream or ice cream if desired. **Yield:** 6 servings.

Black and Blue Cobbler

COOK TIME INDEX

This special index lists every recipe by cook time, so you can quickly find recipes that suit your schedule. Recipes are listed under the minimum cook time. Many have ranges, shown in parentheses, and may cook longer.

INGREDIENT INDEX

*This handy index lists every recipe by food category and/or
major ingredient, so you can easily locate recipes to suit your needs.*

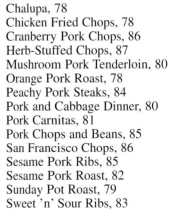